The HUNGER *of the Heart*

A WORKBOOK

The
HUNGER
of the Heart

A Call to Spiritual Growth

A WORKBOOK

Ron DelBene
with Mary & Herb Montgomery

Wipf & Stock
PUBLISHERS
Eugene, Oregon

Unless otherwise indicated, all scripture quotations are from *The New Revised Standard Version* of the Bible, copyright © 1989 by the Division of Christian Education of the National Council of the Churches of Christ in the United States of America. Used by permission of the National Council of the Churches of Christ in the United States of America.

Scripture quotations, identified as RSV are from the *Revised Standard Version* of the Bible, copyright © 1946, 1952, 1971 by the Division of Christian Education of the National Council of the Churches of Christ in the U.S.A. and are used by permission.

Scripture quotations identified as JB are from *The Jerusalem Bible*, copyright © 1966, 1967, and 1968 by Darton, Longman & Todd Ltd. and Doubleday & Co. Inc., and used by permission of the publishers.

Scripture quotations identified as NEB are from the *New English Bible*, © The Delegates of the Oxford University Press and The Syndics of the Cambridge University Press, 1961, 1970. Used by permission.

Scripture quotations identified as PA are from *Psalms Anew*, copyright © 1986 by Saint Mary's Press and used by permission.

Wipf and Stock Publishers
199 W 8th Ave, Suite 3
Eugene, OR 97401

The Hunger of the Heart
A Call to Spiritual Growth: A Daily Workbook for Use in Groups
By DelBene, Ron, Montgomery, Herb, and Montgomery, Mary
Copyright©1995 by DelBene, Ron
ISBN: 1-59752-473-5
Publication date 12/1/2005
Previously published by Upper Room Books, 1995

For all who
have felt
the hunger of the heart

ALSO BY THE AUTHORS

Christmas Remembered
From the Heart

Into the Light Collection:
Into the Light
When I'm Alone
Near Life's End
A Time to Mourn (also on cassette) Study Guide

Times of Change, Times of Challenge Series:
When You Are Getting Married
When Your Child Is Baptized
When You Are Facing Surgery
When an Aging Loved One Needs Care
When You Are Facing a Decision
When You Live with an Illness That Is Not Your Own
When You Have a Decision to Make
When You Want Your Wishes Known: Wills and Other Final Arrangements
When Your Son or Daughter Divorces

Breath of Life Series:
The Hunger of the Heart
The Breath of Life
Alone with God

Video Series
by Ron DelBene

Praying in the Midst of Life:
Our Questions about Prayer
Finding God
Knowing God's Will
Praying the Scripture
Learning the Breath Prayer
Retreating at Any Time

Contents

ABOUT THIS WORKBOOK

SINCE THE HUNGER OF THE HEART WAS FIRST PUBLISHED IN 1983, praise has been generous. People tell me the content is down-to-earth and something they can relate to. As one man put it, "It touches me where I live." Because the stories in the book trigger stories from people's own lives, it has been a popular text in various study groups dedicated to spiritual growth.

Over the years I have often been asked if I'd consider doing a leader's guide for *The Hunger of the Heart*. People who used the book in groups were looking for more structure in their time together and questions that would give a better focus to their discussions. But instead of a leader's guide, my coauthors and I created this workbook designed especially for use in groups. It contains the entire content of *The Hunger of the Heart* as well as daily reflections and exercises.

The time to bring out the workbook had arrived after my video series *Praying in the Midst of Life* was released. The video series includes *Finding God*, which will be viewed at the first meeting of the group. It introduces me and explores the various ways God is present in our lives. The medium of the video enables me to be a part of your group just as so many spiritual seekers have been a part of my life through their friendship and the stories they have shared.

This daily workbook for use in groups provides an avenue for focused reflection whereby you can move more deeply into the life of the Spirit. Doing the daily exercises and sharing your own stories and insights at group meetings opens you to discoveries about yourself and your relationship with God.

Although there are similarities in every spiritual journey, each is as unique as the person making it. At times we may walk blindly. At other times it may seem we have to retrace our steps. But if we persist on the pilgrim's way, we grow in spirit and in truth. At whatever place you may be on your journey, I am privileged to be a part of it. May *The Hunger of the Heart* program enlighten and sustain you as you walk the path that takes you closer to God.

Ron DelBene

GROUP MEETING GUIDELINES

The Hunger of the Heart Workbook has six weekly group sessions and individual daily activities for thirty days. Group sessions may last from forty-five minutes to an hour and a half. (Many people tell me that no matter how long the session, they typically have to cut off discussion.) Those participating in the program are asked to commit themselves to completing the daily readings and reflections and attending the group sessions, understanding, of course, that circumstances sometimes make that impossible.

A group of eight to twelve members is a good size. If the group is too large, it is difficult for everyone to share and participate in the discussion. Because group members will explore and reflect on their faith journey in preparation for the weekly meetings, discussions will likely be more personal and filled with more of their own stories than might be the case in other groups.

Establish when and where you will hold the meetings. If you use the program within a regular church curriculum, the meeting place will probably be predetermined. Otherwise, groups typically meet in church classrooms or parlors or in private homes. When meetings are held in a home, make sure directions to the house are clear and that interruptions (children, pets, telephone) can be kept to a minimum.

There are, however, other possibilities for meeting places. A group of women told me they meet for a long lunch at a local restaurant where they arrange a private room for their meeting. Business people I know gather for an early breakfast and sharing.

For the first meeting you will need a TV and VCR. If the site you've chosen does not have a VCR available, you can hold your first meeting where you have access to one. Thereafter, you may hold meetings elsewhere.

One person from the group can act as the leader for the entire program or assign a leader from week to week. Decide on the leadership format before or at the first group meeting.

If you serve refreshments (food and/or beverages) at the beginning of your time together, do not let it delay starting the meeting. Serve refreshments at the end of the meeting only if you are certain that most of the people can stay most of the time. It does

1

not enhance the group spirit if, on a regular basis, some people have to leave while others are free to stay and continue a lively conversation.

Prayer is an important part of the program. Throughout the week everyone in the group uses the same prayer and scripture; in doing so we leave ourselves open to the power that prayer has to unite us. As we prayerfully enter into the sacred journey of others and share our own, we have the sense of being on holy ground.

Group Leaders:

- Arrange the room ahead of time and have the necessary materials on hand. You may want to have a focus table: a Bible as a reminder that we live in the presence of God's Word, a candle as a reminder that Jesus is the light of the world, flowers or a plant as a reminder that we are all part of a world that is growing and changing.

- Be warm and welcoming to everyone in the group. Name tags help get people comfortable with one another. Even though people may already be acquainted, have name tags anyway in the event someone brings a guest. At the first meeting make name tags encased in plastic and wear them for successive meetings.

- Be willing to share your personal experiences. Sharing an experience of your own encourages others to do the same.

- Encourage everyone to participate. If one or two people dominate the discussion, invite others to contribute.

- Center the discussion on personal experiences. Avoid issues that are unrelated or those that have the potential for becoming only an intellectual debate.

- Use a watch or timer to time silent reflections.

- Keep to the time schedule. If the meeting is running late, get a consensus from the group before continuing beyond the designated time.

- Make these points at every meeting: (1) Each of us has a different view and is at a different place on the journey. (2) There is no one way that God calls a person and no single right way to respond to God's spirit. The closing prayer for each meeting is a way of celebrating both our diversity and our unity.

First Group Meeting

PURPOSE:

To get acquainted and to introduce *The Hunger of the Heart* program.

MATERIALS NEEDED:

- The video *Finding God*, a TV and VCR

- A workbook for each member of the group

- A 3 x 5 index card for each member of the group (See Step 6 below.)

- Watch or timer

- Bible, candle in a sturdy holder, fresh flowers or plant

PREPARATIONS:

- Have the video ready to show.

- Arrange the seating so people can see the video easily. (After the viewing you may want to rearrange the seating in a circle so people can see one another.)

- Create a focus table with the Bible, candle, and plant or flowers. Have the Bible open and the candle lit as people arrive.

PROCEDURE:

➤ 1. Begin with a get-acquainted exercise. Explain that you will begin your time together with one minute of silence (use a watch or timer) during which group members are to think about why they felt called to *The Hunger of the Heart* program. Ask:

- "What hunger of your heart drew you to these sessions?"

After the minute is up, introduce yourself and share the spiritual hunger that brought you to the program. Your response will set the tone for the others, so keep your sharing brief and focused. Turn to the person on your right (or left) and say, "Let's go around the group in this direction."

➤ 2. When everyone has shared, pray this prayer:

> Thank you, God, for bringing us together
> on this spiritual journey.
> Light our way as we travel the road
> that brings us closer to you.
> Be with us to celebrate our triumphs
> and encourage us when we grow weary.
> Wherever we are on the pilgrim's way,
> grant us the grace to feel your presence
> and to know that your love is always with us.
> Amen.

This prayer is the same one you will pray together at the end of the meeting when group members have their workbooks.

➤ 3. Show the video *Finding God.* This video introduces Ron DelBene, author of the book and workbook *The Hunger of the Heart.* (The video takes twenty-one minutes to view.)

➤ 4. Use these discussion questions after viewing the video:

- In what ways do you experience Jesus' presence in the midst of your life?

- As you listened to the people on the video discuss their lives, with whom did you most identify?

➤ 5. If group members do not already have their workbooks, hand them out now. Make these points:

- The workbook has five weeks of daily exercises, each of which includes a reading from *The Hunger of the Heart* and an exercise that pertains to that reading. The daily exercises require twenty to thirty minutes.

- Before beginning the Week One, Day One exercise, read "Called to Wholeness" (p. 6). This reading reviews the video presentation and welcomes members of the group on their spiritual journey.

- Each day's exercise begins with a prayer for a companion on the way. Scripture to pray each day for a week follows. By repeating, or revisiting, a given prayer or scripture, we discover new meanings and new applications to our lives.

- Each day's exercise also has a section called "Reflecting and Responding." Our culture values busyness; we hurry from one thing to another without taking time for reflection. The program emphasizes revisiting prayer and reflecting on our lives as a way to slow our pace and listen more closely to God.

➤ 6. Pass out index cards and ask each member of the group to write his or her name. Place the cards face down and mix them up. Each person then takes a card. People who get their own name draw again. The name on the card is the person they will pray for in the coming week; they then write that name in the space provided in the prayer that begins the week's readings and activities. (Save the cards to reshuffle and reuse each week.)

➤ 7. Invite members of the group to bring a symbol relevant to their journey and put it on the focus table at the next group meeting. In the discussion part of the meeting they will have an opportunity to share their symbol's meaning. It is, however, important to respect that for some people, just bringing the symbol will be all the sharing they care to do.

➤ 8. End with prayer. Use the same prayer that was prayed at the beginning of the meeting. By revisiting the prayer after the sharing that has occurred, the group will likely find new meaning in it. Ask everyone to turn to p. 4 and pray together.

INTRODUCTION

Called to Wholeness

The following reading welcomes you on your journey of spiritual growth. Read it before beginning the workbook exercise for Week One, Day One.

"I invite you to begin thinking of yourself as a pilgrim. . . ."

Why do I always feel there should be something more to life than I am experiencing?

What can I do to make my relationship with God more satisfying?

How can I get my life together?

These are a few of the questions typically faced by people who come to me seeking spiritual direction. I have faced these questions myself, and you probably have as well.

Before we examine the stages of spiritual growth that point to some answers, let's recall what God has in mind for us. Scripture tells us that we are called to be whole people who grow into a deeper balance and union with the parts of ourselves, with other people, and with God. Specifically we are told, "You must therefore be perfect just as your heavenly Father is perfect" (Matthew 5:48, JB).

To be perfect as God is perfect? What an unattainable, even unfair, expectation—an expectation that puts us in what is commonly referred to as a double bind. Such a bind produces an inner dialogue that goes like this:

"I need to be perfect like God."

"But you can't be perfect like God."

"I have to be! It's right there in scripture."

"But you know you can't."

"Even though I know I can't, I must keep trying."

We rid ourselves of the burden caused by this dilemma simply by understanding the meaning of the word *perfect*. In the original Greek, it means "whole," "integrated,"

6

or "together." For most people, this is an entirely new way of looking at their spiritual potential.

Consider your own life. Surely at times you have felt everything was going well, that you were a whole person with your life moving in the proper direction. You were together—integrated in mind, body, and spirit. You were functioning as one, as God intends.

For some people, the potential for a rich spiritual life is damaged because perfection as they understand it is unattainable. Jean was such a person. When she came to see me, she was a wife and mother in her early thirties confronting the issue of always having to be perfect. Worry about being perfect had begun in early childhood. In her journal, Jean wrote about her troubling history:

> I was afraid because I knew what would happen when I brought home a report card with five A's and one B. And it did. The first comment from my father was "Why the B?" So the next grading period I really wanted to "prove" myself. I worked very hard and came home with six A's.

> I was so proud. I knew I had made it. But what was the first response of my father? "Must have been an easy term. Don't let it go to your head. Your class is probably not too smart."

> So there I was! I couldn't win. I remember that time so very well. Maybe that's when I decided that I was a loser. And that was only one instance of many times when I felt I had to live up to something that I couldn't. And I remember crying about that.

> Then I remember the church just adding to that with more about how I needed to be perfect. Wow, I spent my whole life trying to be perfect for my father and never making it, and now God was asking me to be perfect. I was a loser even before I really started.

> When I heard that perfect really means whole or integrated, I got a new lease on life. . . . Suddenly it was like God was a part of my life. My own integration was what he was talking about. At that moment I was just filled with God's love. What freedom! The truth really does make you free.

Whereas mistaken understanding of perfection warps some people's spiritual development, others fall victim to the "ladder mentality." Early in the Christian tradition of spirituality, the ladder became a popular image, symbolizing our growth toward God. Such an image was consistent with the prevailing understanding of God as being "up there" (in heaven) and our being "down here" (on earth). Our responsibility was to get up there to God.

In times past, the ladder image was effective because it was both easy to visualize and to understand. Today we realize that this image does not fully take into account that God has already "come down" and become one of us in the person of Jesus. No longer is there a need to get "up there" to God.

The ladder image also suggested that spiritual growth means rising, step-by-step, to an ever-higher level. (The song "We Are Climbing Jacob's Ladder"—"higher, higher"—is based on the image of the ladder in Genesis 28:12.) We have inherited the idea that the higher we go, the better we are. Certainly it is true that through such activities as prayer, Christian meditation, ministry to others, and study of the scriptures we grow spiritually. But if we hold to the ladder image, we are in danger of being unduly concerned with where we are in relation to others. Are we ahead of someone else? Are others ahead of us? Often we hear judgments, and perhaps even make them ourselves, about our positions on the ladder leading heavenward.

In place of the ladder image, I offer the tree as a more appropriate symbol for our time. At any given moment a tree is complete. If you plant a tree that is two inches in diameter, you don't say, "I planted half a tree today." A tree is a tree no matter what the size. The difference between a tree that is two inches in diameter and one that is twenty inches is that one has been around longer than the other.

So it is with us. God did not create just half a you or half a me. From the moment of our birth, each of us is complete. At times our growth is more rapid than at other times, but at every point in our lives we are whole.

The tree too has periods when growth is more evident. This is apparent when the tree is cut down and the growth rings inside the trunk are visible. Some rings are wide, indicating a time when growth was intense. Other rings are narrow, indicating that growth was slight. We may compare these growth rings to the stages in our spiritual lives. We have growing times when we seem especially close to God. At other times we feel stunted spiritually; we sense very little growth and wonder if we are standing still or maybe even backsliding. Yet even in those seemingly arid times, we are growing.

Martin, whom I first met in his early twenties, was impatient with his spiritual growth and never satisfied with his progress. He found the tree image especially helpful in realizing how a person can be both whole and growing. In one of Martin's journal entries he wrote:

When I heard that I am complete now, I immediately thought, no, I'm not. Then the more I thought about it, the more I see what you mean. I was never pleased with my prayer life, with my walk with God, with the spiritual good I was doing. I always had to be better. Now I see that I am where I am supposed to be. That's a relief. I can begin to enjoy where I am. I know I'm alive and growing, but I'm no longer running.

The call to wholeness is also a call to holiness. For Christians, the two are inseparable. Scripture calls us to

- death and new life (Romans 6:4)

- sin no more (John 5:14)

- pray unceasingly (Ephesians 6:18)

- make peace (Matthew 5:9)

- feed the hungry and clothe the naked (Matthew 25:31-46)

Despite the incidents of violence and human alienation reported daily in the media, I believe that more people than ever hear the call to perfection, the call to wholeness. Look around your own neighborhood or community and you will find people responding to God's call to love and to serve. They join prayer groups, work in soup kitchens, participate in fund drives, and minister to broken hearts and battered spirits.

What about you? Do you have a desire to draw closer to God and to those whose lives you touch? Perhaps as you celebrate another birthday, you feel an inner nudge to focus more on your spiritual life. Or the invitation might become apparent as you work with a therapist, counselor, or spiritual director who helps you discover an untapped dimension of yourself. The call could be as gentle as a whisper while reading the scriptures or as noisy as a shout of outrage when you see an abused child.

As Christians we are called to be whole, called to lead lives of care and concern. So I invite you to begin thinking of yourself as a pilgrim—a person who freely chooses to join in the continuing journey of spiritual growth. In the readings that follow, we will travel that road together.

Happy are the people whose strength is in you!
Whose hearts are set on the pilgrim's way.
(Psalm 84:5, *Book of Common Prayer*, 1979)

Week One, Day One

PRAYER FOR MY COMPANION ON THE WAY:

I give thanks to you, my God, that I do not travel alone on the journey into a deeper awareness of your love. This week I especially remember _____, who is a pilgrim with me. Amen.

CENTER YOURSELF WITH THIS SCRIPTURE:

O God, you are my God, I seek you,
my soul thirsts for you;
my flesh faints for you,
as in a dry and weary land
where there is no water.
Psalm 63:1

Reading for today:

The Awakening Stage

"There must be something more. . . ."

Have you ever been up late watching TV and felt drawn to the refrigerator? You open the door and stare absently inside while all the cold rushes at your feet. You don't know what will satisfy, but finally you pick out something to eat. In a few minutes you are back in the kitchen to get something to drink, thinking that was what you wanted all along. At last you are full—too full—and realize you weren't really hungry or thirsty after all.

The first stage in the journey of spiritual growth is something like that. But instead of a hunger of the senses, it is a hunger of the heart. Many people ignore this crucial moment of awakening because they don't understand what is happening to them. This stage can be both distressing and depressing because no matter what we do, our life just isn't what we once thought it was meant to be. Confusion, unrest, dissatisfaction—these three are the most common feelings at this time.

John, a family man with a comfortable home and a good job in sales, reflected this stage. Although he had a number of reasons to feel fulfilled, he was unhappy with everything about his life. His work no longer challenged him. He ate and drank too much and found himself smoking one cigarette after another. At home, such trivial matters as the slam of a door or a bike left in the driveway caused him to blow up. In John's daydreams he imagined himself escaping to California where he could begin a new life, and this time get it right.

Although John didn't know it yet, he longed for something much more satisfying than the comfortable lifestyle he had worked so hard to attain. He yearned for a deeper relationship with God, yearned for the spiritual dimension that would give meaning not just to his work or home life but to his *entire* life.

As I got to know John better, I found that he really did love his wife and children and enjoyed his job. Looking at the individual parts of his life, he couldn't see anything seriously wrong. Yet in his heart John recognized that something critical was missing. What he had ignored was the call to bring all the aspects of his life into focus around God.

For a moment let's consider what we mean by God. We know that God is our Creator (Genesis 1), that God is love (1 John 4:8), and that God is the One who loves us enough to send Jesus to save us from our sins (John 3:16). Unfortunately, however, these images are difficult to picture. For those who find God abstract and God's presence difficult to image, I suggest thinking of God as did Abba Dorotheus, a spiritual director at the beginning of the seventh century. This is what he said to his students:

> Imagine a circle with its centre and radii or rays going out form this centre. The further these radii are from the centre the more widely are they dispersed and separated from one another. . . . Suppose now that this circle is the world, the very centre of the circle, God, and the lines (radii) going from the centre to the circumference or from the circumference to the centre are the paths of [people's] lives.*

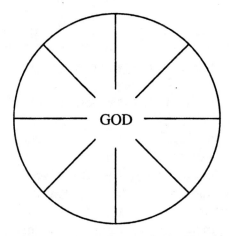

The diagram helps us visualize how we can move either away from or toward God. The choice is ours to make. It also suggests that the nearer we come to God, the closer we come to one another.

Even though we might ignore the hunger of the heart or misinterpret its meaning, it keeps returning. For many people, the first awareness of the hunger is no more than a restlessness, a sense of dis-ease. John's awakening occurred one ordinary morning as he looked in the mirror while shaving and blurted, "There must be something more to life than this!"

*Early Fathers from the Philokalia, translated by E. Kadloubovsky and G. E. H. Palmer (London: Faber & Faber, 1954), 164-65).

For Betty, an accountant, the awakening came in the middle of lunch one day when a friend casually asked, "How do you feel about God?" Later Betty told me that at that moment she felt as though a burden had been lifted from her. Something as simple as a friend's question made her realize that she had to take responsibility for her spiritual life.

In an attempt to offset the hunger of the heart, some people plunge into work or recreation or drugs with such determination that what begins as dis-ease ends up being disease. Workaholism is an example of what happens when someone refuses to acknowledge the importance of developing as a whole person. Marriages deteriorate, children grow up without really knowing their workaholic parent, and interests that would enrich the workaholic's life go unexplored.

Often we experience the hunger of the heart as the desire for something more *out* of life. While there's nothing wrong with that, the hunger of the heart is really a reminder to bring something more *into* life. That something more is an ongoing relationship with God and an ever-deepening faith.

(The awakening stage continues on Day 2.)

REFLECTING AND RESPONDING

Fill in the diagram with aspects of your life: work, church, home life, hobbies, recreation.

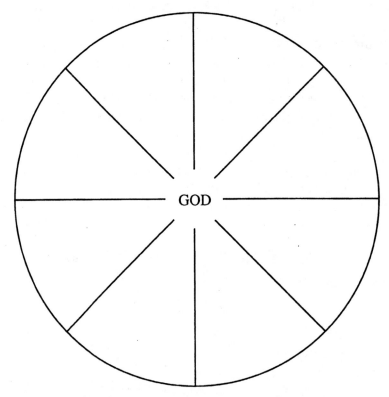

In which areas of your life are you standing still or moving away from God? In which areas are you moving closer to God? Starting from the outer edge of the circle, shade those areas accordingly.

Go, do all that you have in mind,
for the Lord is with you.
2 Samuel 7:3

Week One, Day Two

Prayer for my companion on the way:

I give thanks to you, my God, that I do not travel alone on the journey into a deeper awareness of your love. This week I especially remember _____, who is a pilgrim with me. Amen.

Center yourself with this scripture:

O God, you are my God, I seek you,
my soul thirsts for you;
my flesh faints for you,
as in a dry and weary land
where there is no water.

Psalm 63:1

READING FOR TODAY:

THE AWAKENING STAGE
(CONTINUED)

What I have said thus far may seem to apply only to non-Christians or to Christians whose relationship with God has lapsed. This is not the case. Even a totally committed Christian can experience a sense of dis-ease, a feeling of being dissatisfied and unfulfilled. Why? Because *we may pass through this stage, as well as the other stages on the pilgrim's way, time and time again.*

Remember that spiritual growth is not like a ladder that we climb to be "up there" with God. Rather, our growth is better symbolized by the tree that is complete at all times. As the tree grows in every direction, its roots must go deeper in order to provide stability and supply the necessary nutrients. So it is with us. We too must be growing in many different ways, and the hunger of the heart is our call to grow. It is a sign that God calls us to send our roots deeper and deeper.

A number of years ago I worked for a Christian publishing house and lived in a way that I believed was right for my family and for me. I was in a helping profession and confident that I was doing my job well. In spite of that, I sensed the need to be doing something more. As a result, I chose to become more attentive to my prayer life, which for a time proved very satisfying.

Yet once again I felt the hunger of the heart. Then a struggle began within me. Did God really want me to move to a more simple lifestyle and commit myself to working in the area of spiritual growth? I tried for a time to avoid the question and be satisfied where I was. But God had other plans for me, and no matter what I did, I remained dissatisfied. After a long period of reflection, I surrendered to the fact that this was a time of awakening for me, and I said yes to God. Our family moved and I began work at the Hermitage, a place where people could come to study, reflect, and pray under my guidance. Although you might think that would be the end to my heart's hunger, it was really only the beginning.

In the more than twenty years since then my heart has been hungry at times, and I have moved again through the awakening and other stages to discover more about the next chapter in my life and ministry. These experiences have taught me that the hunger of the heart is never an ending. Rather, it is always a beginning. Either it is an opportunity to let God into our lives for the first time, or it is a chance to move further along the path of spiritual growth with God at our side.

Properly understood, the hunger of the heart is an awakening. At this stage we realize that God calls us to wholeness and fullness of life (Ephesians 1:3-7). When Sharon, an office worker in an auto dealership, came to me, she had narrowly focused her life on a disappointing love relationship—a relationship she thought was the one thing to make her happy. Soon she realized that romantic love was not what she truly needed at this point in her life. In her journal she made this entry:

> *I don't know where all this is leading me, but I know my "heart-burn" continues to increase. I thought a new job would take care of it, but my heart isn't in it. I am functioning. I am doing what needs to be done, but it is a struggle, because I am not committed. I need to be committed, to believe.*

Sharon's moment of awakening was not the first time God had been active in her life. However, for the first time she realized that now she had to respond.

Have you ever experienced—or are you now experiencing—the hunger of the heart? If so, recognize it as God's call to move into a journey in spiritual growth that will involve many stages.

REFLECTING AND RESPONDING

Imagine that the path below is your life. Note times when you experienced new beginnings: birth, school, marriage, job, spiritual experience, counseling, children.

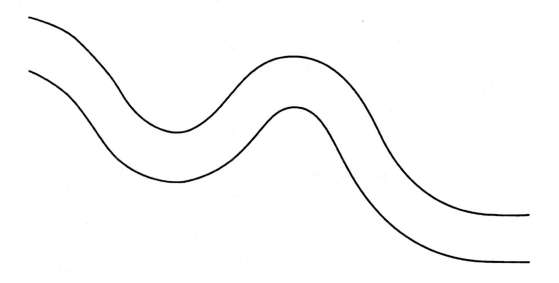

The Spirit is present in all our new beginnings, and in looking back we sometimes see God's action in ways we were unaware of at the time. But at those times of special blessing, like Sharon in today's reading, we are aware *at the time* that God is active in our life and we have a response to make. When have you been aware—at the time—that God was active in your life? Circle those time on your path of life.

> You will decide on a matter,
> and it will be established for you,
> and light will shine on your ways.
> Job 22:28

Week One, Day Three

PRAYER FOR MY COMPANION ON THE WAY:

I give thanks to you, my God, that I do not travel alone on the journey into a deeper awareness of your love. This week I especially remember _____, who is a pilgrim with me. Amen.

CENTER YOURSELF WITH THIS SCRIPTURE:

O God, you are my God, I seek you,
my soul thirsts for you;
my flesh faints for you,
as in a dry and weary land
where there is no water.

Psalm 63:1

READING FOR TODAY:

THE SEEKING STAGE

"I longed to know God. . . ."

Jack's parents divorced when he was a child and left him with many unresolved feelings. Even as a young adult, Jack found it difficult to believe in the permanence of anything. Though recently graduated and newly employed, he realized his heart hungered for something, and a moment of awakening led him to become an active seeker.

When Jack and I first met, he still wore the look of elation so commonly associated with this stage of growth. Seekers are excited about the potential the future holds for them. They see possibilities instead of problems and are eager to get on with the journey. Often they move rapidly from one activity to another, trying to find *the* answer. Jack described what was happening to him during the seeking stage in this way:

> *I began the round of self-improvements: self-awareness with groups, alone, reading... with a deep need for spiritual development. I longed to know God, as I felt that true unconditional love of the Master would free me from turmoil. I longed for the mystical experience.*

If we compare Jack's journal entry with the words of the psalmist, we find that seeking closeness with God unites us with our faith ancestors: "As a deer longs for flowing streams, so my soul longs for you, O God. My soul thirsts for God, for the living God. When shall I come and behold the face of God?" (Psalm 42:1-2)

During the seeking stage, the words *yearning* or *longing* are often used. It is a stage in which there is a sense of wanting something to happen and wanting it to happen *now*. Apprehension may also accompany this yearning; we fear that what we want so much will fail to appear.

When people come to me seeking help in finding God's will for themselves, I share with them that the word *will*, which we translate from the Latin *voluntas*, means "yearning" in both Hebrew and Greek. To ask "What is God's will for me?" is the same as asking "What is God's yearning for me?" To satisfy the hunger of the heart is to satisfy the deep yearning God has awakened within us.

An undefined yearning characterizes the awakening stage. In the seeking stage, the yearning begins to clarify itself, and we have hope that it will be satisfied. Seekers often report feelings of being led and an inability (or unwillingness) to turn back. However we describe the experience, I believe it is the spirit of God calling us closer, loving us as no one else ever can or will. Such love is beyond our human experience, which may be why we are so slow to recognize it.

If we agree that God is like the parent of the prodigal child, yearning for our return to the fullness in and for which we were created, then we begin to see that we are not alone. Nor are we on a journey never traveled before. You and I are but two of the many travelers who have heard the ancient call, sensed the yearning, and set forth. Although the journey is new to us, it is one that all holy people have made. In one of the apostle Paul's letters to the early believers, we glimpse how the Spirit of God draws us to greater wholeness:

> These things God has revealed to us through the Spirit; for the Spirit searches everything, even the depths of God. For what human being knows what is truly human except the human spirit that is within? So also no one comprehends what is truly God's except the Spirit of God. Now we have received not the spirit of the world, but the Spirit that is from God, so that we may understand the gifts bestowed on us by God (1 Corinthians 2:10-12).

(The seeking stage will continue on Day 4.)

REFLECTING AND RESPONDING

Many believe that at the time of our birth God determined what we should do with our lives. Our challenge, then, is to discover what God has in mind for us.
What has been your belief about God's will for you?

_____

_____

_____

_____

How does asking "What is God's *yearning* for me?" change your understanding of God's will or add another dimension to it?

_____

_____

_____

_____

_____

When have you felt led by God's spirit? Describe one such time.

_____

_____

_____

_____

_____

How would you describe your relationship with God at that time in your life?

_____

_____

_____

_____

_____

Be transformed by the renewing of your minds,
so that you may discern what is the will of God—
what is good and acceptable and perfect.
Romans 12:2

WEEK ONE, DAY FOUR

PRAYER FOR MY COMPANION ON THE WAY:

I give thanks to you, my God, that I do not travel alone on the journey into a deeper awareness of your love. This week I especially remember _____, who is a pilgrim with me. Amen.

CENTER YOURSELF WITH THIS SCRIPTURE:

O God, you are my God, I seek you,
my soul thirsts for you;
my flesh faints for you,
as in a dry and weary land
where there is no water.
Psalm 63:1

Reading for today:

The Seeking Stage
(continued)

Seeking is the result of awakening to experience God's spirit. All seekers share this stage and seek according to individual need. Although the inner journey may seem easy at first, seekers soon discover that along with the freedom to make our own decisions, we also have the freedom to make our own mistakes.

Knowing what each stage of spiritual growth involves is helpful, but that knowledge does not ensure a smooth journey. We can expect detours, bumps, and occasional roadblocks. What do we do when these occur? How do we keep on the path we have chosen for ourselves? The answer lies in self-discipline. Some people find the need for discipline unsettling and even threatening. Those who are fearful of assuming personal responsibility for their spiritual growth tend to search for a dogmatic leader or the kind of church that will do their thinking for them. In this area, I advise caution.

Persons at the seeking stage are very vulnerable. Often this vulnerability manifests itself in a wonderful openness toward others. New pilgrims, especially, may project their honesty onto those they meet and may naively put their trust in gurus, teachers, or groups that are subtly seductive. Cults are particularly adept at recognizing seekers and drawing them into physical and mental submission. Though the young are especially vulnerable, more experienced pilgrims are victims as well. During the seeking stage, idealism can be so heightened that the seeker accepts a religious doctrine without question. To examine a new belief system, a seeker can ask these questions:

- Does scripture support this way?

- Does this way seek to be inclusive and not exclusive?

- Has this way been present throughout the history of the Christian church?

- Do followers of this way have a commitment to social justice?

- Does the belief system make a person more loving?

- Does this way help a person focus on the needs of others?

If the answer is yes to all these questions, then the way is probably of God and will lead you on the right path.

While advising caution in the seeking stage, I also want to point out that joyful surprises are in store. The seeker may join a prayer group and find unexpected friendship. Sharing and discussing our spiritual journey with other pilgrims is a particular delight. The support and enthusiasm of others fuel the desire to continue.

During this time, the Spirit leads the seeker to prayer and discipline. To those who ask, "How do I start a disciplined prayer life?" I recommend the breath prayer, which you will discover as part of today's "Reflecting and Responding." The breath prayer does not use other people's words but rather is a short, personal prayer that we discover for ourselves. Persons can say this prayer as easily and naturally as breathing; it lies like a tiny seed within us and when nurtured, grows and flowers into a new closeness with God.

REFLECTING AND RESPONDING

We seek according to our individual need. List those things for which you seek or yearn.

_____

_____

_____

Determine which is your deepest yearning. Draw a star beside it. This yearning will be the heart of your breath prayer.

To discover your breath prayer, turn to page 147.
Write your breath prayer here:

_____

_____

_____

Rejoice always, pray without ceasing.
1 Thessalonians 5:16-17

Week One, Day Five

Prayer for my companion on the way:

I give thanks to you, my God, that I do not travel alone on the journey into a deeper awareness of your love. This week I especially remember _____, who is a pilgrim with me. Amen.

Center yourself with this scripture:

O God, you are my God, I seek you,
my soul thirsts for you;
my flesh faints for you,
as in a dry and weary land
where there is no water.
Psalm 63:1

READING FOR TODAY:

THE LEARNING STAGE

"When the disciple is ready, the teacher appears. . . ."

To move beyond the seeking stage, we must have a teacher. At this point, however, the teacher is not necessarily a person. The teacher may be a book, a movie, a line from scripture, a dream, a waking vision, or some event that we recognize as having special significance for our spiritual growth.

One day I was reading the Gospel for the following Sunday and considering how I would present the core of the message in my next sermon. My usual practice is to read the scripture lessons each day and reflect on them. Then as I go through the week, the meaning shifts and new ideas appear. This particular week was not a good one for me. Each day as I tried to focus on the Gospel, my attention slipped back to a disagreement I had had with Julie, a parishioner. On Friday as I read the story in the quiet of my study, I grumbled aloud, "Who put *that* line in there?" Even though I had read the same scripture four times, I had not seen the words "their minds were closed." On the fifth reading, they stood out boldly.

That day I was the disciple ready to hear. I understood the message and realized that my mind had been closed. If I wanted to resolve the situation I had ignored, I could open my mind by asking Julie to share her thoughts with me.

While in that instance scripture was my teacher, Sandra was at a point in her journey where her teacher needed to be a person. Although Sandra was an intelligent and attractive young woman, she didn't perceive these qualities in herself. She had few friends and no one with whom to share her innermost concerns. She expressed the situation in her journal:

> *What does it matter to me? It matters that there isn't anyone in my life who cares about butterflies. You see, there was this butterfly up on the mountain with me. It had brown velvet wings with orange silk trim, and it did a splendid ballet among the rocks and trees. Then it landed on my shoe and sat still for a long time. But there was no one to share my butterfly.*
>
> *Then Jane, a friend who sensed the depth of my seeking and yearning, suggested I call you. I didn't even know you, or what you did. It seemed*

*that I had tried everything else and was ready to grasp at any straw
that was offered.*

Soon after writing that passage, Sandra acted on her need to meet someone who
would understand her yearning. "At that point I was ready," Sandra told me. "But as I
look back now, I guess I wouldn't have been ready before that."

We can draw a parallel between our spiritual journey and that of the Israelites who
wandered for forty years in the desert. Their yearning and their seeking were, as we read
in scripture, a purification: "For the Israelites travelled in the wilderness for forty years,
until the whole nation, all the fighting men among them, had passed away, all who came
out of Egypt and had disobeyed the voice of the Lord" (Joshua 5:6, NEB).

So it is in our journey. All the internal fighting to get somewhere by our own design,
all the disobedience of knowing the inner voice of God yet choosing to do something
else must pass away. Only when the new creation is within us will we truly be ready to
meet the teacher as did John, a middle-aged counselor who came to see me. A
disciplined runner who was very concerned about his physical fitness, John had just
realized that he had spiritual needs and that he wasn't sure how to meet them. This led
to frustrations that caused problems at home. He became impatient with his family and
made unreasonable demands on his children. John described the struggle in this journal
entry:

> *I had been seeking someone for a long time, but not really. I knew that
> it was inevitable, but it seems now when I look back on it that there
> were parts of me that had to be "cleaned out" before it could come
> about. I guess for the past year and a half, I have been recognizing
> parts of myself which I needed to let go of if I really wanted to grow.*

(The learning stage continues on Day 6.)

Reflecting and Responding

Teachers come in many forms. Listed below are avenues for learning when we are spiritually ready to hear the message. Use this as a guide for listing those special times of learning for you. Be specific in your responses.

People

_____

_____

_____

_____

Events

_____

_____

_____

_____

Books

_____

_____

_____

_____

Movies

_____

_____

_____

_____

Video/Audiotapes

_____

_____

_____

_____

Scripture stories

_____

_____

_____

_____

Scripture passages

_____

_____

_____

_____

Sermons/Homilies

_____

_____

_____

_____

Lectures

_____

_____

_____

_____

Dreams

_____

_____

_____

_____

Waking visions

_____

_____

_____

_____

Other

_____

_____

_____

_____

Learn where there is wisdom.
Baruch 3:14

Week One, Day Six

PRAYER FOR MY COMPANION ON THE WAY:

I give thanks to you, my God, that I do not travel alone on the journey into a deeper awareness of your love. This week I especially remember _____, who is a pilgrim with me. Amen.

CENTER YOURSELF WITH THIS SCRIPTURE:

O God, you are my God, I seek you,
my soul thirsts for you;
my flesh faints for you,
as in a dry and weary land
where there is no water.
Psalm 63:1

Reading for today:

The Learning Stage
(continued)

When the disciple is ready, the teacher does indeed appear. The teacher, however, may not say anything new. Often the message is one we have heard before, sometimes not just once but many times. But now we are spiritually ready—we have, as scripture states, the ears to hear and the eyes to see (Matthew 13:13-17). In reporting his reaction to my direction, John said:

> *Surprisingly enough, you said nothing that I hadn't heard many times, but I suddenly heard it in stereo at high volume. I was surrounded by the words. It was holy ground, and really as if God was speaking. I guess you could say you were a burning bush to me.*

Another example of spiritual readiness occurred when I was teaching a class on unceasing prayer. One of the students, a silver-haired gentleman, kept nodding his agreement as I spoke. Afterward he introduced himself and said, "Tonight was like Pentecost Sunday to me. I heard you talking my language. You don't know how long I've waited to hear someone else speak what I've been saying to myself for years. Thank-you."

Some pilgrims quickly reach the stage at which the teacher appears; while others, like the elderly gentleman in my class, wander in the desert for years. No matter how short or how extended the period of time, it invariably seems too long.

Timothy was a young, obstinate priest whose wanderings, though intense, lasted only a short time. In his journal he recounted an experience that helped him understand this stage of his journey:

> *I was sitting quietly, and the story of Lazarus came to mind, especially the moment when Jesus weeps, sighs, and calls Lazarus forth. Then I felt myself enclosed in a tomb and I found myself removing layers, like blankets. At the first layer, I asked for forgiveness for the self-idolatry. . . . Then came a deeper cover. I was reluctant to touch it, but I did. I pulled it off and a deep sigh came from my heart. Suddenly I was at a door—the same door that I had tried to open before. This time I gave it a hearty yank, and it opened easily. Light fell in upon me immediately. An arm beckoned me to go through the door into this*

unknown world. I did and I felt an embrace throughout my body. Then there was silence.

I see now a new revelation from the story of Lazarus. We are all Lazarus bound up by the wraps of our own death and sin. In the aloneness of our hearts we hear the voice cry, "Come out!" We peel the wrappings that bind us and stumble for the door and into the daylight of life and the loving arms of Jesus.

Timothy's new awareness prepared him to continue his journey. His recollection of the experience helps us see that when we are ready, the teacher appears. Whether the teacher be a person, a book, a movie, a line from scripture, a dream, a waking vision, or another event that reshapes our thinking is unimportant. What matters is that we are ready. Then when we hear God call our name, we, like Samuel, have the opportunity to answer, "Here I am" (1 Samuel 3:4).

Reflecting and Responding

When have you had the eyes to see and the ears to hear something familiar in a new way? How did it come about—through something you witnessed or read or heard? Write about your experience.

_____

_____

_____

_____

Blessed are your eyes, for they see,
and your ears, for they hear.
Matthew 13:16

PREPARATION FOR THE GROUP MEETING

In the group meeting, the leader will invite you to share experiences you've had so far on your spiritual journey. Use these questions to help review your week.

- Which story, paragraph, or line in the reading did you find especially meaningful? Mark it so you can find it easily.

- Have there been other times in your life when you went through the stages discussed in this week's reading? If so, when?

- Read through the Reflecting and Responding exercises from the past week. Do you find any of your responses surprising? If so, why?

- As you did the Reflecting and Responding exercises, did you have an insight or remember a past discovery? Or—as you revisit the activity now—does an insight or discovery occur to you? If so, take a moment to write about it, or capture it in a collage or sketch on a separate piece of paper.

_____

_____

_____

_____

- Remember to bring this book to the group meeting. You may want to refer to something you read or wrote during the week.

Second Group Meeting

Purpose:

To share experiences of the past week and to honor one another's journey of the spirit.

Materials needed:

- Name tags if people are not yet acquainted
- Bible, candle with a sturdy base, plant or fresh flowers
- Watch or timer
- 3 x 5 index card for each member of the group with his or her name on it (Make new cards if they were not saved from the previous week's meeting.)

Preparations:

- Arrange the seating so people can see one another easily.
- Create a focus table with the Bible, candle, and plant or flowers. Have the Bible open and the candle lit as people arrive.

Procedure:

If anyone brought a symbol to share, place it on the focus table. (Those who brought symbols will have an opportunity to tell the group about them during the discussion time. Others may wish to describe something that is symbolic for them.)

➤ 1. Begin by praying together this scripture that all have prayed throughout the week:

> O God, you are my God, I seek you,
> my soul thirsts for you;
> my flesh faints for you
> as in a dry and weary land
> where there is no water.
> Psalm 63:1

➤ 2. Follow with three minutes of silence. (Use a watch or timer.) Ask that the group members reflect on their experiences during the week:

- a particular learning, insight, or rediscovery;

- a story from the text with which they especially identified;

- God's presence in their lives this week.

➤ 3. Initiate group sharing. Invite anyone who has something to share to do so. If no one responds, use the following questions to stimulate discussion. It's not necessary to cover all the questions. Because different people relate to different questions, it's helpful to read them all and then wait for someone to begin. At some meetings, the group may spend the entire discussion time on just one question.

- How have you experienced God's presence this week?

- What particular learning or insight did you gain?

- With which person's story in the readings for this week did you most identify?

- What was your experience in discovering your breath prayer?

End the discussion ten minutes before the end of your meeting. This allows time for picking new prayer companions and the closing ritual. So as not to end the discussion abruptly, give a five-minute warning by saying, "We have five minutes of discussion time left."

➤ 4. Pick new names for prayer companions. Place the 3 x 5 cards face down and mix them up. Each person draws a name; those who get their own draw again. Ask group members to write their new prayer companion's name in their workbooks.

➤ 5. Begin the closing ritual with a minute of silence. (Use your watch or a timer.) After the silence, ask everyone to look around the group with an awareness of how blessed we are to share our journey of the spirit with one another. (Give a brief moment to look around.) Ask the group to turn to this prayer in their books. Together pray:

Thank you, God, for bringing us together
on this spiritual journey.
Light our way as we travel the road
that brings us closer to you.
Be with us to celebrate our triumphs
and encourage us when we grow weary.
Wherever we are on the pilgrim's way,
grant us the grace to feel your presence
and to know that your love is always with us.
Amen.

Week Two, Day One

Prayer for my companion on the way:

I give thanks to you, my God, that I do not travel alone on the journey into a deeper awareness of your love. This week I especially remember _____, who is a pilgrim with me. Amen.

Center yourself with this scripture:

I am always aware of your presence;
you are near, and nothing can shake me.
And so I am full of happiness and joy,
and I always feel secure.

You will show me the path that leads to life;
your presence fills me with joy,
and your help brings pleasure forever.
Psalm 16:8-9, 11, PA

The Relief, Anger, Fear Stage

"But my God, I am so fearful. . . ."

At times the journey seems all uphill, but the recognition that a teacher can help us brings relief. This sense of relief means that we are moving along on our journey and have reached a new stage—that of relief, anger, fear. The relief we felt at finding a teacher turns out to be transitory, however; and as Emily's story illustrates, we often experience anger and fear.

At twenty-six, Emily had a history of being rejected. Even though she had been hurt, she refused to be bitter, choosing instead to continue a search for a community where she would find acceptance. Her most recent rejection had occurred when she told some members of her church about a vision she had experienced. A man in the group immediately suggested that she needed counseling. Although Emily probably could have benefited from such help, she had expected understanding from the group, not advice. She believed that other Christians would understand and appreciate her feelings; and when they didn't, she once again felt the sting of rejection.

I happened to meet Emily on the rebound. Fortunately, she was still open to God's love and eager to make sense of her confusing experiences. Keeping a journal helped her gain a new perspective as we see in this excerpt from her early writings:

> *I have been going around for the past few years, just searching out someone or someplace where I could know that I belonged. This morning at church, I came home. It has been a long journey, but now I am home. What a relief. I can quit looking.*

Her great relief was short-lived. A few weeks later, an anxious and upset Emily came to my church office and asked if she could see me. I invited her in and had no more than closed the door when she shouted, "Where were you when I needed you? Why did it take me so long to find this place? Why can't the church have more people who care?"

Emily's words rolled like ocean waves in a storm. I had never before met anyone so angry about spending so much time seeking and not finding. At last she slumped into a chair. After a deep sigh, she said quietly, "I'm sorry. I don't know why I'm so angry at you. It just all seems so cruel."

I assured Emily that although she might feel her reaction was confused and inappropriate, it was not unusual. The relief felt at finding a teacher often gives way to anger as seekers reflect on having had to wait so long.

Then I mentioned to Emily that she was also likely to experience fear, the third emotion that can be expected at this stage of spiritual growth. Emily drew back and laughed nervously. "You must have read my mind," she said. "Just last night I was talking with a friend about how exciting it was to find this new support for my walk with God, and I found myself feeling afraid. I couldn't understand it. It was as if I wouldn't be in control."

A review of the relief-anger-fear stage shows how logically one emotion follows the other:

- We yearn for something with our whole being.

- We find it and are relieved to know that at last we are not alone.

- Then we become angry that it took so long to reach that point.

- Finally, we experience fear that now we may have to do something.

When people are at the relief-anger-fear stage of their journey, I often share an excerpt from Bob's journal. Though young in years, Bob was old in experiences. He had been a heavy drug user and dropped in and out of one subculture after another. Spending time at the Hermitage was, he thought, just going to be another experience to add to his repertoire. God, however, had other designs as we see in this entry:

> *There is a gentling process taking place. I am very much at peace and feel good about myself. After so long not feeling good about myself—this is a nice change. I am not trying so hard to have an exceptional experience or hear the voice of God or see an exceptional vision. I am just trying to be. I am only trying to have patient expectations and to let this time heal me. But, my God, I am so fearful that something really will happen!*

> *What will I have to do now that I really have found someone and someplace that challenges me and takes me seriously? I think that maybe I was better off running around wildly to keep my mind off the call from God that I kept hearing. But I don't remember ever feeling this afraid, even during some of the bad trips on drugs. Fear. Now maybe I'll have to do something. Maybe that's why the apostles were so often fearful.*

41

When Emily finished reading this journal excerpt, she put it down and said simply, "I know what he means."

(The relief, anger, fear stage continues on Day 2.)

REFLECTING AND RESPONDING

Often our fears cause anxiety that manifests itself in many ways. One way to banish fear is to bring it into the light where you can examine and deal with it.

I am afraid of

Write your fears on the rays of the sun. Each time you write a fear, pray: "Grant me insight into my fear, O God" or "O God, may your light dispel my fear."

Week Two, Day Two

PRAYER FOR MY COMPANION ON THE WAY:

I give thanks to you, my God, that I do not travel alone on the journey into a deeper awareness of your love. This week I especially remember _____, who is a pilgrim with me. Amen.

CENTER YOURSELF WITH THIS SCRIPTURE:

I am always aware of your presence;
you are near, and nothing can shake me.
And so I am full of happiness and joy,
and I always feel secure.

You will show me the path that leads to life;
your presence fills me with joy,
and your help brings pleasure forever.
Psalm 16:8-9, 11, PA

READING FOR TODAY:

The Relief, Anger, Fear Stage
(CONTINUED)

Many people stay in a given stage for months or even years. For them, spiritual growth is rather like beginning a business but never really tending to it. This was true of Dolores, a priest in her early forties who kept so busy with the problems of her congregation that she avoided her own needs. She thought that coming to the peacefulness of the Hermitage was simply going to be a rest—a time away from the pressures of her work. The afternoon Dolores arrived, she said it was almost like coming to the ivy-covered cottage of her childhood imaginings. Here was a place to be alone with her dreams, her prayers, and her Bible.

But the next morning Dolores was far from peaceful. When she met me at the door, her face was tense and stern. We sat opposite each other in the prayer room and Dolores looked at me with blazing eyes. "The whole institutional church stinks!" she cried. "Why did I have to come this far and wait this long to find a place to be alone and pray?"

Dolores's anger was a familiar and understandable part of this stage. In middle age, she was frustrated by the realization that she had put off her personal spiritual growth. At first she tried to find someone to blame, which is a usual response. We like to believe that our failure to grow is the fault of our parents or teachers or the pressure of work or the denomination in which we grew up, all of which do affect us. However, instead of trying to place blame, how much wiser to assess how we were molded, where we are now, and how we are going to proceed on our journey of the spirit.

As time went on in her retreat, a calmer Dolores began to look ahead and see new possibilities. In her journal, she wrote:

> *Am I ready to hear God? Ready to do whatever God asks me? Rather frightening! I know myself so well. Will it be something I don't want to give up? I'm afraid. . . .*

The way I experience the relief, anger, fear stage is best described in a family story that happened when our children were young. Near our home was a water flume, a huge playground slide built into a hillside. Water gushed down the slide and flume riders zoomed round and round the curves on plastic mats before splash landing in a pool at the bottom. Secretly I wanted very much to ride the flume. When I shared this desire with my children, they soon convinced me it was a great idea, so we set a time for a family outing.

Standing at the top of the flume I had two realizations: the flume was much higher than I thought it would be, and I faced the unexpected. *Going down? Not me!* But there I stood, unwilling to retreat and scared to go forward. I got angry at myself for wanting to do such a foolish thing. It was an irrational moment. I knew that thousands had made this trip safely and I would too, but. . . .

The line kept getting shorter and shorter. Then it was my turn. Tense as a stretched rubber band, I put the mat down and the flowing water whisked me away. My little mat went so fast that I felt totally out of control. With my hands frozen in a grip, I pulled the front of the mat up, not realizing that doing so gave me even less control. In total panic I spun completely around, forgetting even that there was water at the bottom. Suddenly I made a splash landing and laughed. How easy it was!

So often our life with God is that way. We want to climb to the heights, have the vision, and enjoy the ride, so to speak. But how hard it is to give control to God and let be what will be.

Not everyone experiences the relief-anger-fear stage in the same way. Depending upon our personality and background, the intensity of each emotion varies. But in this crucial stage of growth we are confronted with the reality as old as the Exodus. Like the Israelites we are relieved to be saved from bondage, then angry that it took so long, and eventually fearful about what the future may hold.

REFLECTING AND RESPONDING

- The first step to moving beyond a fear is confronting it.

- The second step is taking actions that will help us see the fear for what it is.

- The third step is surrendering control to God and letting be what will be.

One thing I fear as I travel the journey of the spirit:

_____

_____

_____

Action(s) I can take to overcome that fear:

_____

_____

_____

_____

All things can be done for the one who believes.
Mark 9:23

Week Two, Day Three

Prayer for my companion on the way:

I give thanks to you, my God, that I do not travel alone on the journey into a deeper awareness of your love. This week I especially remember _____, who is a pilgrim with me. Amen.

Center yourself with this scripture:

I am always aware of your presence;
you are near, and nothing can shake me.
And so I am full of happiness and joy,
and I always feel secure.

You will show me the path that leads to life;
your presence fills me with joy,
and your help brings pleasure forever.
Psalm 16:8-9, 11, PA

READING FOR TODAY:

THE DOUBTING STAGE

"Doubts are of different kinds and usually come in bunches. . . ."

What happens when doubts arise on your spiritual journey? Although doubting and questioning can happen at any stage, it is most likely to occur after encountering a teacher and being challenged by God through that teacher to enter into the journey more actively. At this point we may feel reluctant to go further. We are tempted to dig in our heels and stay put or even return to the familiarity of a previous stage.

The doubting stage follows the relief-anger-fear stage and is a natural outgrowth of fear. While participating in the process of growth and movement into God's loving power, we eventually wonder whether we are doing the right thing. This new territory has unfamiliar landmarks, and we are understandably wary.

We can liken this stage to an experience our family had years ago on a visit to New York City. From the 102nd floor of the Empire State Building to the second basement of the subway, it is a city of sharp contrasts and immense size. The number of people seated on the main floor of one Broadway theater we attended was greater than the entire population of our hometown!

I especially remember our family's first excursion on the subway. We knew where we wanted to go and had seen on the map of the system which trains to take. Still, there was a bit of hesitation about "really doing it." Finally we made our decision and began the trip. Every time the train stopped, I nervously checked to make sure we were still on the right line. We completed that first trip successfully and two others as well. After that third trip, I felt secure about where we were going and even gave directions to fellow tourists.

We can draw parallels between that experience and our journey into a deeper relationship with God. As we begin the journey, the territory is strange and we wonder if we are going in the right direction. Awed by the experience, we proceed with trepidation. What's happening may even overwhelm us. This is natural when moving from the familiar to the unfamiliar.

Just as the subway map helped me find my way in the city, this book's intention is to help you find your way through the stages of growth. Soon you will be familiar with the signposts and recognize where you have been, where you are, and where you are going. When that happens, a glow of understanding will give you the confidence to point the way for others who are just beginning the journey.

On every journey doubts arise. They are different kinds and usually come in bunches:

- Am I on the right track?

- Does anyone else take God seriously?

- Whom should I really trust?

- Isn't God too awesome for me to comprehend?

- Is there truly a journey?

- Haven't I just been standing still?

- Why me?

(The doubting stage continues on Day 4.)

REFLECTING AND RESPONDING

Which of the preceding questions do you ask yourself?

_____

_____

_____

_____

A question I ask myself that is not included here:

_____

_____

_____

_____

I find myself asking these questions when . . .

_____

_____

_____

_____

Lead me in your truth, and teach me.
Psalm 25:5

Week Two, Day Four

PRAYER FOR MY COMPANION ON THE WAY:

I give thanks to you, my God, that I do not travel alone on the journey into a deeper awareness of your love. This week I especially remember _____, who is a pilgrim with me. Amen.

CENTER YOURSELF WITH THIS SCRIPTURE:

I am always aware of your presence;
you are near, and nothing can shake me.
And so I am full of happiness and joy,
and I always feel secure.

You will show me the path that leads to life;
your presence fills me with joy,
and your help brings pleasure forever.
Psalm 16:8-9, 11, PA

READING FOR TODAY:

THE DOUBTING STAGE
(CONTINUED)

If we let them, doubts will clutter the path and prevent us from moving ahead. It then becomes easy to fall back to an earlier stage that we understand and accept or, as Ellen did, get bogged down right where we are.

At age thirty-four, Ellen was the wife of a successful executive and the mother of three children. Aside from being a busy homemaker, she played an active role in her community. Amid the busyness of her life, however, Ellen heard her name called much the way Samuel had (1 Samuel 3:1-10). She decided to take some time for reflection. She came to the Hermitage where she entered these thoughts in her journal:

> *This morning I got up and wondered to myself, what am I doing here? I am panicked in a sense. I began to think of all the people who would think that spending time in solitude in a little place in the middle of a wooded area was crazy. Yet I feel that this is where God is calling me at this point.*

A few days later, Ellen had seen through the doubts and recognized them for what they were—defenses against moving ahead in her journey. She went on to write:

> *Now I see more clearly why I had not come to the Hermitage before this time. I was not ready. Moreover, I don't think I would have been able to move through the tremendous doubts that I had the other night. I think I would have gotten out of here and gone home. I see now that the doubts about what I was doing here and the fear that I would probably be thought crazy were all my defenses. Probably for the same reason I brought all my needlework and books and art supplies. I remember thinking I had to bring enough to do in case I got restless. I see now that the restlessness was fear and a defense against hearing the voice of God in the silence of being alone.*

Sometimes we are simply not ready to move further along the path of spiritual growth. At other times, we are certain the time is right, and still we decide not to go. Excuses that get expressed as doubts are endless. Perhaps the most destructive doubt is one expressed by a young student who said, "I just can't imagine that God would choose me and want me as a friend. I mean, why would God care about me? Who am I?"

Why is it so hard to accept that God loves us unconditionally? Why do we feel we have to earn God's love? We may find partial answers in our upbringing. Children commonly feel the need to earn parents' love and to win friends' and neighbors' approval. A culture that tells us we must perform to be rewarded reinforces the message we got in childhood. Thus we do the things we know will get us the affirmation we desire. We may dress for the approval of others. We may follow a career path to satisfy a parent. We may marry or befriend a person we know we can please. Not surprisingly, in our spiritual life we also look for ways to earn God's love. And how damaging it is to that relationship when we begin to doubt that God truly loves us.

But God does love us, loves us freely, with no strings attached. God's love is a gift. All we need do is accept it!

When doubts arise, it is helpful to talk with someone. This role is one the spiritual directors have always filled. If no such guide is available to you, try meeting with someone who has made the journey previously. Another help at this stage is to search out reading material on the struggles of others as they sought to know the fullness of God's love. Above all, remember that doubting is a stage we all go through, and that it too shall pass if we are dedicated to the journey we have begun.

Reflecting and Responding

Feeling loved and encouraged helps us believe that God is active in our lives. But what about those times when we feel rejected or abandoned? Scripture assures us that "all things work together for good for those who love God" (Romans 8:28). Everything we experience—the doubting, the pain, the joy, the grace-filled moments—we can all use to nourish the soul and draw us closer to God, our source of strength and hope.

Use the stepping stones on the following page to reflect on your life. Note times that you felt accepted and encouraged. Also note times of rejection and abandonment. Remember that this is for your eyes only; share only if you feel comfortable doing so.

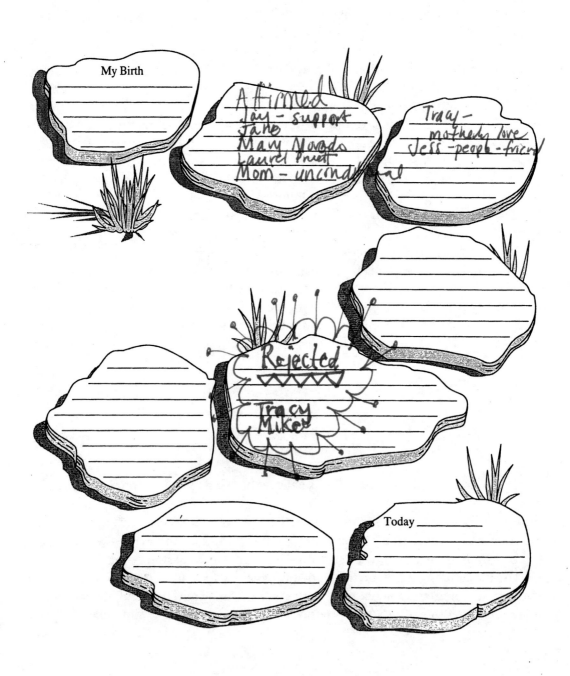

Week Two, Day Five

Prayer for my companion on the way:

I give thanks to you, my God, that I do not travel alone on the journey into a deeper awareness of your love. This week I especially remember _____, who is a pilgrim with me. Amen.

Center yourself with this scripture:

I am always aware of your presence;
you are near, and nothing can shake me.
And so I am full of happiness and joy,
and I always feel secure.

You will show me the path that leads to life;
your presence fills me with joy,
and your help brings pleasure forever.
Psalm 16:8-9, 11, PA

READING FOR TODAY:

THE TESTING STAGE

"I really had to check it out. . . ."

Two clergymen who attended my presentation of prayer at a workshop in the Midwest approached me afterward. I knew from their whispers and skeptical glances that something had unsettled them. Finally one of them said in a halting fashion, "That was . . . ah . . . very interesting, and we were wondering where you took your theological training."

The name tags these clergymen wore indicated they were from a section of the country where it was commonly believed that a certain seminary dean practically "sat at the right hand of God." Smiling to myself I offhandedly said, "Oh, at Marquette University, the same place where Dean _____ got his degree."

My answer brightened the men's faces, and they began speaking excitedly about my presentation. Having passed their test for authenticity, they were now eager to speak in more detail about their own spirituality.

Testing or verifying the authenticity of someone we look to for guidance is a necessary step in the process of spiritual growth. When we find someone with whom we "click" or who "speaks our language," we want to be sure that person is qualified. Although it is important to be cautious, as were the two clergymen, it is also important that we not measure a person solely on the basis of degree or position. To test for authenticity, I suggest using this question: Does the person's lifestyle reflect an application of his or her teachings?

In my early years as a pastor, I had great difficulty with people's testing my authenticity. It frustrated me when I was asked, "Do you possess the Spirit?" or "Have you been born again?" or "Have you experienced 'this' or 'that' program?" Although I could answer the questions positively, I felt I wasted time with explanations when we could move ahead. Not until an incident in Kansas City did I truly appreciate how necessary it is to test authenticity.

To reach Kansas City, I had flown halfway across the continent. A late arrival meant I had to eat on the run and rush to the convention where I gave three talks of a very intense nature. At the end of my final presentation, a woman I guessed to be in her mid thirties came forward and asked, "Do you walk in the Spirit?"

Tired and wearing thin, I snapped, "I believe that when a person walks in the Spirit, others who also walk in the Spirit have no need to ask. They know."

The woman pulled back, her smile gone. "I . . . I'm sorry," she said. "But you see, I've just begun to walk in the Spirit and am still learning so much. Religion and prayer are all new to me, and I'm a bit scared. I'm trying hard to be sure I listen only to people who will be able to help me. I felt you were speaking just to me today, and I had to check it out."

Oh, to take back my brusque response! Drawing a deep breath, I apologized and explained how hectic my day had been. Then we talked at length about how it feels at the beginning of our journey. By the time our conversation ended, the woman was smiling again, and I had a better understanding of the importance of testing for authenticity.

(The testing stage continues on Day 6.)

Reflecting and Responding

An old expression is "Practice what you preach." The updated version is "Walk your talk." Either expression is a yardstick to test for authenticity—both our own and that of our mentors.

Think of three people who meet such a standard of authenticity for you. Write their names in the spaces indicated. Beneath each name give one example of this person's walking her or his talk.

Name_____

_____

_____

_____

Name_____

_____

_____

_____

Name_____

_____

_____

_____

Be doers of the word, and not merely hearers.
James 1:22

Week Two, Day Six

PRAYER FOR MY COMPANION ON THE WAY:

I give thanks to you, my God, that I do not travel alone on the journey into a deeper awareness of your love. This week I especially remember _____, who is a pilgrim with me. Amen.

CENTER YOURSELF WITH THIS SCRIPTURE:

I am always aware of your presence;
you are near, and nothing can shake me.
And so I am full of happiness and joy,
and I always feel secure.

You will show me the path that leads to life;
your presence fills me with joy,
and your help brings pleasure forever.
Psalm 16:8-9, 11, PA

READING FOR TODAY:

THE TESTING STAGE
(CONTINUED)

Whenever we move into a new area of experience, our tendency is to look for people with similar experiences. Through sharing, we authenticate what has happened to us. Over the years I have discovered the importance of sharing more and more of my own journey. Other pilgrims can then compare their experiences with mine, and in a very real sense, test me to see if I am real from their point of view. At a conference I conducted in Florida, I discovered that the teachers are not the only ones who get tested for authenticity.

This conference was attended mainly by medical professionals. After an all-morning session on spirituality, I asked the participants to spend some quiet time reviewing their lives and matching the stages of growth to their individual journeys. When we regathered later in the afternoon, a dentist from New York said, "I have another way of looking at the whole issue of testing authenticity." Although he acted hesitant, I sensed that he was overflowing with feelings he needed to express. With a little encouragement, he agreed to share his insights with the group. This is what Tom had to say:

> I don't know if I can verbalize what I want to, but I'm aware that I'm not testing the speaker's authenticity as much as I'm testing my own. This conference was recommended to me by a friend I trust, so I really didn't worry about you. I figured you were for real.

> But now I find I'm measuring myself against you to see how authentic I am. If you are an example of what it means to be a person of prayer and open to the God-call to wholeness, then how am I in relation to you? Not that I have to be like you. But I have to know that someone is what I think I want to be and that I can see within them some measure of what I want to be. I really am testing my own authenticity rather than testing yours. Your authenticity is not an issue with me, but mine is.

Tom's honest self-evaluation prompted me to caution him about the Christian competition game. Although we all need models for comparison, we are not out to become "better than" other Christians.

As Christians, we strive to follow Jesus, so it would be a mistake to turn responsibility for our spiritual growth over to any leader who might in effect become our messiah. We do, however, need role models who confirm our hopes that it is possible to become something more than we are. For one brief conference, I provided that model for Tom, and I feel certain that he is now a model for others.

I recall how Freida, a woman with whom I shared a spiritual director-directee relationship, discovered the part a role model played in her journey. One day she called and asked me a question. When I replied, "I don't really know," Freida quipped, "What! Ron DelBene doesn't have the answer?" There was a pause before she added, "Something significant just happened. I'll have to think about it and get back to you."

A few days later, Freida called back. She made some small talk before saying, "You're on the path too, aren't you?" I smiled to myself, reminded of my own moments of doubting, seeking, and receiving insights. "Yes, Freida," I said. "I too am on the path."

When Freida next spoke, her voice was warm with appreciation. "Well, thanks for letting me make you my messiah for a while," she said. "I never would have moved into the journey as I have if I hadn't thought you were all together and finally finished. I guess I had to believe for a time that perfection was possible. Now, I think I can be on the journey with you."

As Freida discovered, it helps to have someone against whom to measure ourselves at certain points during our journey. Unfortunately some people remain at this stage, spending a lifetime trying to be like someone else and constantly measuring themselves against that person. Some teachers, dealing with their own ego needs, encourage this dependency. The guideline is to accept help when we need it from those who can give it but always to remember that no one of us has arrived spiritually. We are all travelers on a journey that takes us deeper into the life of the Spirit.

Reflecting and Responding

As we travel the path of our spiritual journey, we find people who support and encourage our efforts to move deeper into the life of the spirit. Use the diagram to celebrate those people.

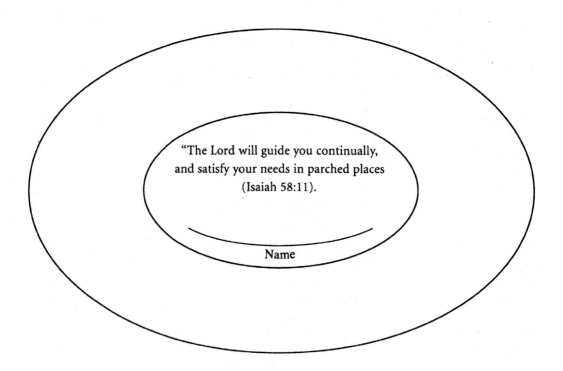

"The Lord will guide you continually, and satisfy your needs in parched places (Isaiah 58:11).

_____
Name

- Write your name in the space indicated.

- In the outer oval note who or what has encouraged you on your journey so far: people, events, situations, books.

PREPARATION FOR THE GROUP MEETING

In the group meeting, the leader will invite you to share experiences you've had so far on your spiritual journey. Use these questions to help review your week.

- Which story, paragraph, or line in the reading did you find especially meaningful? Mark it so you can find it easily.

- Have there been other times in your life when you went through the stages discussed in this week's reading? If so, when?

- How have you been more aware of God's action in your life?

- Read through the Reflecting and Responding exercises from the past week. Do you find any of your responses surprising? If so, why?

- As you did the Reflecting and Responding exercises, did you have an insight or remember a past discovery? Or—as you revisit the activity now—does an insight or discovery occur to you? If so, take a moment to write about it, or capture it in a collage or sketch on a separate piece of paper.

_____

_____

_____

_____

- Remember to bring this book to the group meeting. You may want to refer to something you read or wrote during the week.

Third Group Meeting

Purpose:

To share experiences of the past week and encourage one another on the journey of the spirit.

Materials needed:

- Name tags if they seem necessary

- Bible, candle with a sturdy base, plant or fresh flowers

- Watch or timer

- 3 x 5 index card for each member of the group with his or her name on it (Make new cards if they were not saved from the previous week's meeting.)

Preparations:

- Arrange the seating so people can see one another easily.

- Create a focus table with the Bible, candle, and plant or flowers. Have the Bible open and the candle lit as people arrive.

Procedure:

If anybody brought something that symbolizes their journey of the spirit, they may place it on the focus table. (Those who brought symbols will have an opportunity to tell the group about them during the discussion time. Others may wish to describe something that is symbolic for them.)

➤ 1. Begin by praying together this scripture that all persons have prayed throughout the week:

I am always aware of your presence;
you are near, and nothing can shake me.
And so I am full of happiness and joy,
and I always feel secure.

You will show me the path that leads to life;
your presence fills me with joy,
and your help brings pleasure forever.
Psalm 16:8-9, 11, PA

➤ 2. Follow with three minutes of silence. (Use a watch or timer.) Ask that the members of the group reflect on their experiences during the week:

- a particular learning, insight, or discovery;

- a story from the text with which they especially identified;

- God's presence in their lives this week.

➤ 3. Initiate group sharing. Invite anyone who has something to share to do so. If no one responds, use the following questions to stimulate discussion. It's not necessary to cover all the questions. Because different people relate to different questions, it's helpful to read them all and then wait for someone to begin. At some meetings the entire time for discussion may be spent on just one question.

- How have you experienced God's presence this week?

- What particular learning, insight, or discovery did you gain?

- With which person's story in the text did you most identify?

- How did you feel as you reflected on fear in your life?

End the discussion ten minutes before the close of your meeting. This allows time for picking new prayer companions and the closing ritual. So as not to end the discussion abruptly, give a five-minute warning by saying, "We have five minutes of discussion time left."

➤ 4. Pick new names for prayer companions. Place the 3 x 5 cards face down and mix them up. Each person draws a name; those who get their own draw again. Ask group members to write their new prayer companion's name in their workbooks.

➤ 5. Begin the closing ritual with a minute of silence. (Use your watch or a timer.) After the silence, ask everyone to look around the group with an awareness of how blessed we are to share our journey of the spirit with one another. (Give a brief moment to look around.) Ask the group to turn to this prayer in their books. Together pray:

Thank you, God, for bringing us together
on this spiritual journey.
Light our way as we travel the road
that brings us closer to you.
Be with us to celebrate our triumphs
and encourage us when we grow weary.
Wherever we are on the pilgrim's way,
grant us the grace to feel your presence
and to know that your love is always with us.
Amen.

Week Three, Day One

PRAYER FOR MY COMPANION ON THE WAY:

I give thanks to you, my God, that I do not travel alone on the journey into a deeper awareness of your love. This week I especially remember _____, who is a pilgrim with me. Amen.

CENTER YOURSELF WITH THIS SCRIPTURE:

Yahweh, you are gracious and compassionate,
slow to anger and full of love.
Yahweh, you are good to all
and have compassion on all your works.
All your works give you thanks, O God,
and your faithful ones bless you.
Psalm 145:8-10, PA

READING FOR TODAY:

THE DISCIPLINE STAGE

"There is a positive side to discipline. . . ."

For most of us, discipline has a negative connotation. The very word creates butterflies in the stomach and a tightness in the shoulders because it suggests a painful experience. For me, one such experience involved a second grade teacher I will call Miss Sutter who taught penmanship in a room where every wooden desk had an inkwell. I can still recall my tight grip on the pen and my fingers cramping as I painfully formed endless rows of A's , B's, C's and on through all twenty-six letters of the alphabet. The result of Miss Sutter's demanding standards was that I, along with everyone else in her class, learned to write at least reasonably well.

Even though we may have unpleasant memories involving discipline, we know we can acquire no skill without being attentive to the learning process. If the word *discipline* calls forth negative feelings, I suggest substituting *attentiveness*. Being attentive is more than just paying attention. It means "to be faithful," and faithfulness is the key to discipline as it relates to our spiritual journey. We are called to be faithful people, and the idea of faithfulness is the theme of God's call to the Hebrew leaders as well as to the people themselves: "You shall be my people and I will be your God" (Ezekial 36:28, JB). Although the people failed to be faithful, God did not turn away from them; God's faithfulness is forever.

To be faithful means to submit to another or "to place oneself under another." When that kind of submission is linked with love, we are not a slave to the other but a friend (John 15:14-16). Discipleship too is related to this kind of submission in that as disciples we place ourselves under the teaching of another. Disciple and discipline come from the same root word.

Disciples are *attentive* to the words and actions of the teacher. As Christ-followers, we are called to put on the mind of Jesus and place ourselves under the new law of love. Loving as Jesus loved lets people know we are his disciples. Jesus often refers to the "good and faithful servant" and reminds us that to be faithful and attentive is to be disciplined.

Examples of the disciplined life are all around us. People who run and are faithful to running come to a point at which they cease being people who run; they are *runners*. People who play the piano and are faithful in their practice at some point are no longer .

people who play; they are *pianists.* Likewise, people who pray and are attentive and faithful in praying reach a point at which they undergo a change. They are *pray-ers,* but more than that, they *are* prayer.

(The discipline stage continues on Day 2.)

Reflecting and Responding

Find a creative way to be attentive to your prayer life. Examine a typical weekday and note the times when you are attentive to prayer.

6:00–9:00 AM

_____

_____

_____

_____

9:00–Noon

_____

_____

_____

_____

Noon–3:00 PM

_____

_____

_____

_____

3:00–8:00 PM

_____

_____

_____

_____

8:00–12:00 PM

_____

_____

_____

_____

The breath prayer you discovered on Week 1, Day 4 enables you to develop a new and deeper awareness of God's presence, when you cannot set aside specific times for prayer.

In everything by prayer and supplication
with thanksgiving let your requests
be made known to God.
Philippians 4:6

Week Three, Day Two

PRAYER FOR MY COMPANION ON THE WAY:

I give thanks to you, my God, that I do not travel alone on the journey into a deeper awareness of your love. This week I especially remember _____, who is a pilgrim with me. Amen.

CENTER YOURSELF WITH THIS SCRIPTURE:

Yahweh, you are gracious and compassionate,
slow to anger and full of love.
Yahweh, you are good to all
and have compassion on all your works.
All your works give you thanks, O God,
and your faithful ones bless you.
Psalm 145:8-10, PA

The Discipline Stage
(continued)

How much easier it would be if spiritual growth happened as naturally as grass growing or trees budding in the spring. But we know it doesn't happen that way. Although we begin life as spiritual beings, growth demands effort on our part. Scripture tells us: "I know all about you: how you are neither cold nor hot. I wish you were one or the other, but since you are neither, but only lukewarm, I will spit you out of my mouth" (Revelation 3:15-16, JB).

Despite the call to go beyond the average—to be something more than lukewarm—many people do not respond. A Flemish writer on spiritual matters, Jan Van Ruys-broeck, referred to Zaccheus as someone willing to go beyond the average. In his fourteenth-century writings, Van Ruysbroeck suggested that we must be like Zaccheus, who ran ahead of the crowd and climbed a tree so that he might see Jesus.

The problem with many people in the discipline stage is that they are not certain which tree to climb! Although they recognize the need to be more attentive to their spiritual life, they see a forest ahead of them where each tree has a different sign: "Study," "Fast," "Minister," "Pray," and so on. Instead of climbing any one tree, people at this stage hold back, sure that some day they will recognize the ideal way to grow spiritually.

Barbara found not knowing which tree to climb to be a problem both in her professional and spiritual life. Throughout her seminary training, she felt called to serve in youth ministry. Once ordained she immediately found herself deeply involved with programs, planning, and people. Parents and teachers expected her to know what would "work" with young people. Barbara drove herself to become aware of new thinking and trends so that she could be on top of her job. Then came a day when she wondered what her wide-ranging attempts had accomplished. This is what she confided in her journal:

> *It seems that the greatest difficulty with the students is that this week it's one approach and next week it's another. They're in it for the hype they can get. . . . And then I became aware that I didn't have anything concrete to give them either. I was just like they were. While I was in the seminary, there was a particular approach I used to develop my spiritual life. Then when I got out, I was involved with something else and have never settled into any form of discipline for myself.*

When people stop jumping from method to method and program to program, they are more at peace. Whatever facet of spiritual development they pursue gets their full attention and they soon reap the rewards of a more focused and disciplined life. I have found this to be especially true among people who give their faithful attention to prayer. I don't mean the rote praying of memorized prayers, although that type of prayer is important. The kind of prayer I mean is something we become. This faithful attitude leads us to pray even when we don't feel like praying (Romans 12:12). It is what we do in response to a God who is ever-faithful. This is positive discipline, and something Anthony found very difficult.

Anthony was an investment banker who at age thirty-six was a financial success but who found it difficult to be attentive to his spiritual needs in a regular, ever-deepening way. For several years he had been like a hungry child, heaping more on his spiritual plate than he could handle. He began a serious reading program, allowed it to drop by the wayside, felt guilty, and then began the cycle all over again by trying something new. Finally he realized what was happening and considered a simpler approach. As he explained in his journal, focusing on prayer seemed a reasonable goal:

> *I've been talking a good game for years about this religion stuff, but now I see prayer related to all areas of my life. I have been going to "get into" a discipline for a long time now. The idea of being faithful strikes me the most. I have a high regard for faithful people. Maybe it's time for me to be one.*

What about you? Are you ready to see the positive side of discipline? Do you feel the desire to be more attentive to some aspect of your spiritual growth? If so, why not decide on an area and begin focusing on it now? Start with something at which you will experience success, remembering that you run a mile before you run a marathon.

REFLECTING AND RESPONDING

Again referring to the image that Abba Dorotheus used (page 12), imagine that the circle is your life. God is the center, and each one of the radii is an aspect of your life: work, family, social, exercise, church, learning, recreation (add others applicable to you). Starting from the outer edge of the circle, shade in the wedges to the extent that you are aware of God's presence in a given area. There is no right or wrong, good or bad response.

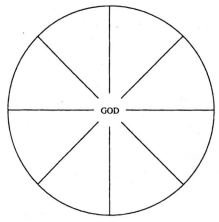

Now examine what you have done.

In what area of your life do you experience the greatest awareness of God's presence?

_____

_____

In what area(s) do you want a greater awareness of God's presence?

_____

_____

How might that happen?

_____

_____

The Lord searches every mind,
and understands every plan
and thought.
1 Chronicles 28:9

WEEK THREE, DAY THREE

PRAYER FOR MY COMPANION ON THE WAY:

I give thanks to you, my God, that I do not travel alone on the journey into a deeper awareness of your love. This week I especially remember _____, who is a pilgrim with me. Amen.

CENTER YOURSELF WITH THIS SCRIPTURE:

Yahweh, you are gracious and compassionate,
slow to anger and full of love.
Yahweh, you are good to all
and have compassion on all your works.
All your works give you thanks, O God,
and your faithful ones bless you.
Psalm 145:8-10, PA

READING FOR TODAY:

THE REBELLING STAGE

"I feel bored and want to give it all up. . . ."

After Elaine recognized that discipline could be a positive force in her life, she became more committed to her spiritual growth. Prayer was at the heart of the changes she experienced, and she was consistently attentive to it. At the time, she was in her midthirties and felt she was "on her way" spiritually. But all that changed abruptly as we see in one of her journal entries:

> *I woke up one morning and thought, I bet there are 35,999 people in our town of 36,000 who are not going to get out of bed this morning to sit in prayer, read the scripture, and reflect upon God's word. Then why am I? Who do I think I am? I mean, really, why do I think I am so special?*

Because Elaine had felt so buoyed by her disciplined life, she was not prepared for the rebelling stage of her journey. Just as she had begun to appreciate the joy of her growth in faith, her resolve to be a faithful person was challenged.

As we enter this stage, there seems to be a tormentor inside us who is intent on raising doubts about the validity of our journey. It is as though we approach that moment of being altogether and suddenly things come apart. The tormentor reflects a lifetime of doubts about our potential. This inner voice has always reminded us of our shortcomings:

"You're not really smart."

"You're not really attractive."

"You're not really lovable."

"So of course, you're not really called to be holy."

The rebelling stage is that point on the journey where we may remember (sometimes in the most vivid detail) all our sinful actions. We are the star in a past that replays itself like a movie that portrays only our weaknesses, failures, and shortcomings. The message we receive is that our sins could never be totally forgiven and that we could not be special to God.

At this stage in our journey, the teacher or the guide who previously had been so helpful may appear to have feet of clay and be unworthy of our confidence. We begin to look for faults in that person so we can justify saying there is nothing to all this religious stuff. Or we hedge by saying that if there is something to it, we can find the way ourselves.

Shannon reached the rebelling stage after she had already made several U-turns on her faith journey. Each time this happened, she had the confidence to continue seeking and persisted in her attempts to be attentive to her faith development. But when she got to the rebelling stage, she became depressed. She entered this in her journal:

> *I would describe this as a spiritual low point. I feel tired and depressed and actually seem to will not to pray. . . . Very uptight and tense. I am empty. I feel just bored and want to give it all up.*

The rebelling stage is not a pleasant one to be in. Yet despite the doubts and the despairing moments, it is a positive part of the journey. How can this be? The positive aspect is that it is the beginning of self-revelation, yet our inner voice urges caution because we are about to meet the person God created us to be. That person has often been hidden from view, and we are anxious about the discoveries we will make. It is understandable that we might want to rebel.

(The rebelling stage continues on Day 4.)

REFLECTING AND RESPONDING

The better we understand ourselves and our needs, the closer we can come to God. Complete the brief self-inventory below. Don't forget qualities of the Spirit. (For example: I can be trusted . . . be a friend . . . be compassionate . . . keep a confidence. . . .)

I can

_____

_____

_____

_____

I like

_____

_____

_____

_____

I've never tried, but I'd like to

_____

_____

_____

_____

When I have the chance, I can probably be good at

_____

_____

_____

_____

No one knows it, but I think I'm especially

_____

_____

_____

I praise you, for I am fearfully
and wonderfully made.
Wonderful are your works.
Psalm 139:14

Week Three, Day Four

Prayer for my companion on the way:

I give thanks to you, my God, that I do not travel alone on the journey into a deeper awareness of your love. This week I especially remember _____, who is a pilgrim with me. Amen.

Center yourself with this scripture:

Yahweh, you are gracious and compassionate,
slow to anger and full of love.
Yahweh, you are good to all
and have compassion on all your works.
All your works give you thanks, O God,
and your faithful ones bless you.
Psalm 145:8-10, PA

READING FOR TODAY:

THE REBELLING STAGE
(CONTINUED)

Hamilton was a lawyer who began to question his journey and where it was taking him. Although he thought of himself as rational and even-tempered, others perceived him as unfeeling—something Hamilton was not aware of. He was a highly disciplined person in all areas of his life, so when he made up his mind to pray regularly, he was faithful to his commitment. His breath prayer, which formed the foundation of his prayer life, was "Father, let me feel your love." Because of his nature, Hamilton expected to see results.

After praying his prayer for about six months, Hamilton came to see me to talk over an uneasiness he felt about his spiritual journey. It was obvious to me that significant changes were taking place within him. I asked how he was getting along at home and how he was relating to people at work.

"My wife mentioned something about my being more gentle, especially with the kids," Hamilton said. He went on to explain that the legal secretaries had talked about his being so pleasant and that it seemed as if he was just back from a vacation. When I asked what he thought about these comments, Hamilton said, "I'm afraid people might take advantage of me if I'm too gentle or pleasant." A bit later in the conversation, he said, "The main reason I wanted to see you is that my breath prayer is beginning to change. I used to always say, 'Father, let me *feel* your love,' and now I'm saying, 'Father, let me *know* your love.' "

"What's the matter?" I asked. "Are you beginning to feel God's love?"

Hamilton immediately caught my meaning. "Yeah, I guess so," he admitted, "but it's scary!"

Having opened himself to healing and wholeness, Hamilton now had to deal with what had occurred: His prayer was being answered. He was becoming the even-tempered person he had believed himself to be but was not. His wife and the people at the office recognized the change before he did, and Hamilton found this scary. And no wonder, because it is. When wholesome, newly discovered aspects of ourselves emerge, we often try to hold on to the familiar. What God asks is that we move into new growth and move on.

In my own journey, I experience the rebelling stage most often in those moments throughout the day when a window of time opens. Often it is in those five or ten bonus minutes when someone is late for an appointment, or I arrive early for a meeting and am sitting in the car in the parking lot. During those times I listen to this conversation in my head:

"Great, you've got this time to get some work done."

"Come on, take some time to be aware of God's presence."

"But you could get one more thing done in these few minutes."

"Yes, and that one thing could be sitting in silence for a minute or two and being attentive to God."

And so it goes. I wish I could say that I always take the time right then and there to be still and aware of what it means to be in God's presence. But after more than thirty years of trying to be attentive to God, at times I fill the window of time with the "one more thing" that needs doing. Then I shrug my shoulders, smile to myself, and admit the constant challenge to be faithful to a life of prayer.

In the rebelling stage, the two greatest temptations are to go it alone or to drop out. Because it is difficult to admit our weaknesses to another person, the trap is set. Often we step right in and drop back to an earlier stage.

When we feel the rebel within, we must confide in someone who understands the pilgrim's way. Often we feel that we are in a static place, a place of no movement. The person in whom we confide may help us see that at this point God asks us to continue reaffirming our dependence on God. Recognizing that we are dependent on God and not on ourselves is both a fearful and a freeing experience, and one against which we rebel.

Just as all the previous stages have been temporary, so too is the rebelling stage. Each time I am at this place on my journey, I recall something a friend shared with me: "Remember that, when shifting from low to high gear, you have to go through neutral."

REFLECTING AND RESPONDING

If you are doing this exercise in the morning, think back to yesterday. If you are doing it in the evening, think of the past day. Were you in situations in which windows of time opened up? Note in the window illustrations when the free time occurred and how you used it.

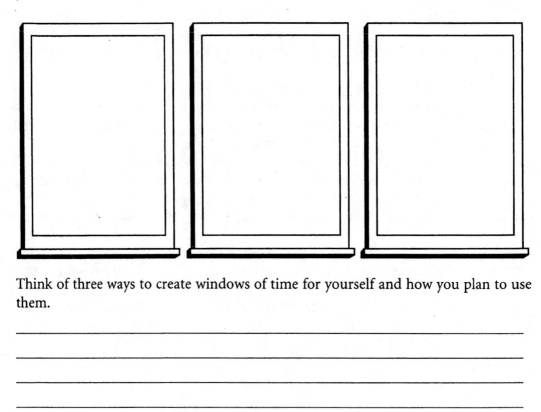

Think of three ways to create windows of time for yourself and how you plan to use them.

_____

_____

_____

_____

For everything there is a season,
and a time for every matter under heaven.
Ecclesiastes 3:1

Week Three, Day Five

Prayer for my companion on the way:

I give thanks to you, my God, that I do not travel alone on the journey into
a deeper awareness of your love. This week I especially remember
_____, who is a pilgrim with me. Amen.

Center yourself with this scripture:

Yahweh, you are gracious and compassionate,
slow to anger and full of love.
Yahweh, you are good to all
and have compassion on all your works.
All your works give you thanks, O God,
and your faithful ones bless you.
Psalm 145:8-10, PA

READING FOR TODAY:

THE URGED-ON STAGE

"Whatever it is that is moving me won't let me stop. . . ."

A friend of mine once had a car with a broken gas gauge. Because he was never sure how much gas was in the tank (especially after his children drove the car) he would find himself sputtering to a halt in the middle of an important trip. My friend's experience has an application to our spiritual journey. The urged-on stage is one in which we figuratively run out of gas and can go no further alone. In order to move on, we must have the help and encouragement of others.

Sam was at a point in his faith journey where he found himself stalled. He was a construction worker with a wife and four children, and he lived with a lot of stress. Layoffs, which are so common in his field, were a particular concern. Sam's faith-life was a great source of comfort to him, but a time came when he began to neglect his spiritual growth. He described the experience this way:

> On the surface, each day seemed too busy for me to find time to pray. A week passed. What a loss! Looking back, I know I could have cut my lunch time short. But not praying on Saturday and Sunday was pure stubbornness on my part. My mind tried to convince me that I didn't need to pray anymore. Nevertheless, my heart wanted to be aware of God's presence. My whole being yearned for the experience. I was driven to begin again.

In Sam's case, the Spirit was at work, urging him on when he could not continue alone. His experience reminds me of Psalm 42 in which the psalmist says, "Why are you cast down, O my soul, and why are you disquieted within me? Hope in God; for I shall again praise him, my help and my God" (Psalm 42:11).

Like Sam, many of us are urged on by the Spirit, but we also may benefit from the help of individuals and groups. Throughout the week we can have private time with God, whereas Sunday provides an opportunity to share our faith with others. In our churches, we and the other members of our faith community celebrate our faith and are urged to go forth and do God's work in the world.

Not all people, however, respond favorably to being urged on through communal celebration. A few are even antagonized by it. At one time or other, I suspect every member of the clergy has heard a variation of these remarks spoken to me by a parishioner. "I want you to know," she said sternly, "that I come to church on Sunday for my time with God. I come to worship, not to celebrate. And your celebration is getting in the way of my worship. Sunday is the only time I can really pray, and I want my time with God alone!"

I am never quite sure how to respond to such people. I don't think they understand that even though we may pray in private, prayer is a communal action. We are not saved as isolated individuals to enter a private kingdom of God; we are called in community and invited to the wedding banquet. I have noticed that people who want only to be alone with God often have small smiles, rarely laugh, and are not only alone but lonely. Although these people may act pleasant, anger seems to live just beneath the surface. Their fierce independence sets them apart, and I wonder if they ever have the need to be urged on. Perhaps their beliefs are so fixed they never suffer from doubts, but I don't believe that to be the case.

(The urged-on stage continues on Day 6.)

REFLECTING AND RESPONDING

The illustration on the following page represents your spiritual journey since beginning *The Hunger of the Heart* program. Indicate where you have needed urging on. To the right of the path note the person, event, scripture, or whatever it was that encouraged you to continue the journey. To the left of the path note anyone you have helped along the pilgrim's way and what you did to urge that person on.

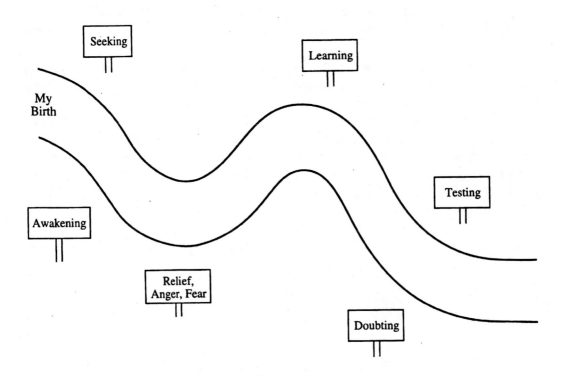

Whenever we have an opportunity,
let us work for the good of all.
Galatians 6:10

WEEK THREE, DAY SIX

PRAYER FOR MY COMPANION ON THE WAY:

I give thanks to you, my God, that I do not travel alone on the journey into a deeper awareness of your love. This week I especially remember _____, who is a pilgrim with me. Amen.

CENTER YOURSELF WITH THIS SCRIPTURE:

Yahweh, you are gracious and compassionate,
slow to anger and full of love.
Yahweh, you are good to all
and have compassion on all your works.
All your works give you thanks, O God,
and your faithful ones bless you.
Psalm 145:8-10, PA

READING FOR TODAY:

THE URGED-ON STAGE
(CONTINUED)

In some churches, parishioners consider it solely the pastor's responsibility to do the urging. Though unfair for a number of reasons, it primarily deprives church members of an opportunity to share the Christian experience. When I was a pastor in a small Alabama town, I experienced what happens when parishioners assume responsibilities. They flower! They open up and share the beauty that God has placed within them.

As pastor of this parish, I saw how praying with and for one another during the week created a joyous unity that was apparent before, during, and after shared worship. Time and time again throughout my years of pastoring I have seen that people who have a common experience in Bible study or a weekend retreat or a social outreach project also have a great desire to celebrate in community. Through their celebration they encourage and support one another.

I see an analogy between what takes place in a loving faith community and a phenomenon that occurs in nature. When geese fly in formation, the lead position changes often. The lead goose drops back to the side where the air passes easily and another moves to the cutting edge of the formation. When one goose is hurt or weak and drops back, at least one other goose goes along. But for me the most fascinating aspect of all this is that geese honk encouragement from behind. They urge one another on.

On your spiritual journey, you may sometimes feel that you are not flying with the support of others but that you are a solitary person going it alone. Even though it may seem that way, such is not the case. Others are making the journey also. They are, so to speak, "honking from behind," urging you on.

At times the lines separating the stages of spiritual growth blur. For instance, while feeling anxious and rebellious, we might also be urged to move ahead. My good friend Bill is an example of this ambivalence. He is a doctor who has been on the journey for years, and through both the peaks and valleys of his life he remains a faithful pilgrim. Here is one of his journal entries:

> *I know why I cannot stop now. I've known for some time that whatever has been moving me in the direction I have been going in the last four years is more powerful than I am. Whatever is moving me won't let me stop. The pages continue to be turned and the pilgrim travels on.*

Reflecting and Responding

After three weeks of praying daily for another member of your group—and knowing that someone is praying for you—what are your feelings about being part of a supportive faith community? Write a prayer that incorporates your thoughts and feelings.

Rejoice with those who rejoice,
weep with those who weep.
Romans 12:15

PREPARATION FOR THE GROUP MEETING

In the group meeting, the leader will invite you to share experiences you've had so far on your spiritual journey. Use these questions to help review your week.

- Which story, paragraph, or line in the reading did you find especially meaningful? Mark it so you can find it easily.

- Have there been other times in your life when you went through the stages discussed in this week's reading? If so, when?

- How have you been more aware of God's action in your life?

- Read through the Reflecting and Responding exercises from the past week. Do you find any of your responses surprising? If so, why?

- As you did the Reflecting and Responding exercises, did you have an insight or remember a past discovery? Or—as you revisit the activity now—does an insight or discovery occur to you? If so, take a moment to write about it, or capture it in a collage or sketch on a separate piece of paper.

_____

_____

_____

_____

_____

- Remember to bring this book to the group meeting. You may want to refer to something you read or wrote during the week.

Fourth Group Meeting

Purpose:

To share experiences of the past week and encourage one another on the journey of the spirit.

Materials needed:

- Name tags if they seem necessary

- Bible, candle with a sturdy base, plant or fresh flowers

- Watch or timer

- 3 x 5 index card for each member of the group with his or her name on it (Make new cards if they were not saved from the previous week's meeting.)

Preparations:

- Arrange the seating so people can see one another easily.

- Create a focus table with the Bible, candle, and plant or flowers. Have the Bible open and the candle lit as people arrive.

Procedure:

If any persons bring something that symbolizes their journey of the spirit, they may place it on the focus table. (Those who brought symbols will have an opportunity to tell the group about them during the discussion time. Others may wish to describe something that is symbolic for them.)

➤ 1. Begin by praying together the following scripture that persons have prayed throughout the week:

> Yahweh, you are gracious and compassionate,
>
> slow to anger and full of love.
>
> Yahweh, you are good to all
>
> and have compassion on all your works.
>
> All your works give you thanks, O God,
>
> and your faithful ones bless you.
>
> Psalm 145:8-10, PA

➤ 2. Follow with three minutes of silence. (Use a watch or timer.) Ask that the members of the group reflect on their experiences during the week:

- a particular learning, insight, or discovery;

- a story from the text with which they especially identified;

- God's presence in their lives this week.

➤ 3. Initiate group sharing. Invite anyone who has something to share to do so. If no one responds, use the following questions to stimulate discussion. It's not necessary to cover all the questions. Because different people relate to different questions, it's helpful to read them all and then wait for someone to begin. At some meetings the entire time for discussion may be spent on just one question.

- How have you experienced God's presence this week?

- What particular learning or insight did you gain?

- Would you be willing to share the prayer you wrote yesterday?

- What practical ways have you found to be attentive to God throughout the day?

End the discussion ten minutes before the close of your meeting. This allows time for picking new prayer companions and the closing ritual. So as not to end the discussion abruptly, give a five-minute warning by saying, "We have five minutes of discussion time left."

➤ 4. Pick new names for prayer companions. Place the 3 x 5 cards face down and mix them up. Each person draws a name; those who get their own draw again. Ask group members to write their new prayer companion's name in their workbooks.

➤ 5. Begin the closing ritual with a minute of silence. (Use your watch or a timer.) After the silence, ask everyone to look around the group with an awareness of how blessed we are to share our journey of the spirit with one another. (Give a brief moment to look around.) Ask the group to turn to this prayer in their books. Together pray:

Thank you, God, for bringing us together
on this spiritual journey.
Light our way as we travel the road
that brings us closer to you.
Be with us to celebrate our triumphs
and encourage us when we grow weary.
Wherever we are on the pilgrim's way,
grant us the grace to feel your presence
and to know that your love is always with us.
Amen.

Week Four, Day One

Prayer for my companion on the way:

I give thanks to you, my God, that I do not travel alone on the journey into a deeper awareness of your love. This week I especially remember _____, who is a pilgrim with me. Amen.

Center yourself with this scripture:

Lead me in your truth and teach me,
for you are the God of my salvation;
for you I wait all the day long.
Be mindful of your mercy, Yahweh,
and of your steadfast love,
for they have been from of old.
Remember not the sins of my youth,
or my transgressions;
according to your steadfast love remember me,
because of your goodness, Yahweh!
Psalm 25:5-7, PA

READING FOR TODAY:

THE CONFESSION STAGE

"I had to stop, look honestly at these things, and confess. . . ."

Our entire journey is a process of putting off the old person and putting on the new (Ephesians 4:22-24). Often along the path of that journey we recognize we have sinned and try to make amends. But when we reach the confession stage, we view our sinfulness in much more detail. We see our past, not through a glass darkly, but clearly—perhaps even through a magnifying glass. When Jane reached this stage, she described her experience this way:

> *All of a sudden it was like traveling down the highway and seeing my past on the billboards in front of me. I couldn't go on. I had to stop, look honestly at these things, and confess that I had sinned.*

For some time, Jane had been aware of great changes in her spiritual life. Her experience reminded her of John the Baptist's calling for repentance because the kingdom of heaven was at hand (Matthew 3:2). When we experience that "at-hand-ness," we know that the old has been—or is about to be—stripped away, and something new will take its place.

This experience of the new's replacing the old calls to mind something that happened near our home. We live in a rural area, and a nearby interstate was under construction for several years. During that time, we saw the nearby mountains made low and the valleys brought up (Isaiah 40:4). We watched the crooked old road made straight. This same process takes place in our spiritual lives. When we come to the confession stage and work our way through it, we feel more at ease on our journey, more balanced. God makes the mountains and valleys even. Crooked parts of our lives, which once made us afraid to see what was around the corner, are made straight.

In the confession stage, we reflect on how good God has been to us and feel humbled by our lack of appreciation. This is how Jane wrote about it:

> *As I look more and more on the way that God has called me from so many places and brought me into his loving care and direction, I am overwhelmed that God would care for me.*

Wrongdoings which previously may have seemed inconsequential, now become significant. We feel compelled to make amends for those occasions when we believe we have sinned. Some of those sins are easily pinpointed: times when we lied, stole, or cheated. Others are not recognized so easily.

In Old English, "sin" is an archery term that means missing the target. As we progress along the pilgrim's way, we become much more aware of the target that is God's love. All those times we have missed the target give us an accumulated sense of failure and feelings of sinfulness that aren't so easily identified.

The recognition that we need to set things right—need to confess our sins—may be the most painful part of our journey. So painful, in fact, that we try to avoid it. Frequently people backtrack from this stage, putting off that which we are called to do. What they fail to appreciate is that God's love and mercy are boundless. No story lets us know this more surely than the prodigal child who returns home to the welcoming parent (Luke 15:11-32). God is such a parent, waiting to enfold us with warmth and forgiveness.

(The confession stage continues on Day 2.)

REFLECTING AND RESPONDING

List old things that have been made new in your life: a damaged relationship revitalized, a negative attitude turned positive, a dormant spirituality starting to blossom, a sin acknowledged and forgiven. The list will be personal, and you will share only to the extent that you feel comfortable doing so.

_____

_____

So if anyone is in Christ, there is a new creation:
everything old has passed away;
see, everything has become new!
2 Corinthians 5:17

Week Four, Day Two

Prayer for my companion on the way:

I give thanks to you, my God, that I do not travel alone on the journey into a deeper awareness of your love. This week I especially remember _____, who is a pilgrim with me. Amen.

Center yourself with this scripture:

Lead me in your truth and teach me,
for you are the God of my salvation;
for you I wait all the day long.
Be mindful of your mercy, Yahweh,
and of your steadfast love,
for they have been from of old.
Remember not the sins of my youth,
or my transgressions;
according to your steadfast love remember me,
because of your goodness, Yahweh!
Psalm 25:5-7, PA

READING FOR TODAY:

THE CONFESSION STAGE
(CONTINUED)

How we seek forgiveness is an individual matter. You may prefer to do it privately with Jesus as your guide, remembering that

> If anyone does sin, we have an advocate with the Father, Jesus Christ the righteous; and he is the atoning sacrifice for our sins, and not ours only but also for the sins of the whole world. (1 John 2:1-2)

Instead of confessing privately, you may find it consoling to seek forgiveness with the help of another person through the ritual of "confessing" or "making yourself whole before God." As part of my ministry, I am humbled to share those issues of life that people consider sin. Often it is with fear and trepidation that someone says to me, "Please, hear my confession before God." The fact that as an ordained priest I can act in the name of the community of believers and that God has given that power (John 20:22-24) is an immense relief to those seeking forgiveness in this way. It's a profound experience to have a hand placed upon your head and to hear that you are forgiven. Indeed, touch is often more healing than words.

At this point I want to stress that the confession stage is a call to do more than seek forgiveness for a particular sin. It is a call to alter radically not just a part of your life but your whole life, to look at yourself and see what causes you to miss the mark. To accomplish this I recommend a life review. This will take no more than an hour, and in the process you are likely to discover a pattern of turning away from God's love.

Sally set out to do a life review, and only part way through her list she had this insight:

> *The more I remembered, the more aware I became of a pattern in my life. It seems that I was always motivated by envy. And I think that envy has really been the basic issue with me since a very young age.*

Envy had led Sally to sin in many ways, but it is doubtful she would have understood this without making the list and seeing a pattern of behavior. Her life review gave her the insight she needed to make a basic change that would affect all areas of her life.

Paul too had an insight while doing his life review. At thirty-eight, he was a busy husband and father of two children who was more concerned about others than about himself. After doing a life review, he described his new awareness this way:

> *I must reorder my entire life. I need to get out of debt and free myself of a terrible burden. I need to practice seeing Jesus in everyone. I need to care for my body with diet and exercise. I need to do more praying. I need to bridle my anger. How long this enormous struggle within me will go on, I don't know. It's like washing out a stubborn stain. I became aware of the truth. I must change.*

(The confession stage continues on Day 3.)

REFLECTING AND RESPONDING

The exercise for today is a life review. When doing your life review, use the next page or—in the interest of privacy—write on a separate sheet of paper.

1. Find a quiet place that assures your privacy.

2. Sit in a comfortable position and take two or three deep breaths to relax yourself.

3. Pray the Lord's Prayer or read a favorite passage from scripture. Psalm 139 is appropriate. In the final two lines the psalmist simply and sincerely invokes God's help in looking inward:

> Search me, O God, and know my heart;
> test me and know my thoughts.
> See if there is any wicked way in me,
> and lead me in the way
> everlasting.
> Psalm 139:23-24

4. List instances when you *consciously* chose to miss the mark as a child of God. Either begin in the present and go back year by year, or begin with your earliest memories and move forward. It is not necessary to go into elaborate detail nor to relive the experiences. Your list is simply a way to focus on your life experiences up to the present. (If other people are involved, do not name them. In the event the list is lost, their privacy would be violated.)

_____   _____

_____   _____

_____   _____

_____   _____

_____   _____

When you have finished your review, put your list aside and celebrate that God's love has been present with you. Tomorrow we will look at what others have done to acknowledge their forgiveness. You will then decide what to do with your list and how you might celebrate God's forgiving love.

If we confess our sins, he who is faithful

and just will forgive us our sins and

cleanse us from all unrighteousness.

1 John 1:9

Week Four, Day Three

Prayer for my companion on the way:

I give thanks to you, my God, that I do not travel alone on the journey into a deeper awareness of your love. This week I especially remember _____, who is a pilgrim with me. Amen.

Center yourself with this scripture:

Lead me in your truth and teach me,
for you are the God of my salvation;
for you I wait all the day long.
Be mindful of your mercy, Yahweh,
and of your steadfast love,
for they have been from of old.
Remember not the sins of my youth,
or my transgressions;
according to your steadfast love remember me,
because of your goodness, Yahweh!
Psalm 25:5-7, PA

READING FOR TODAY:

THE CONFESSION STAGE
(CONTINUED)

The list you made yesterday of times you "missed the mark" can be put to use in several ways. Some people find it helpful to go alone into a quiet church and take the time to read through the list and turn it over to God. Still others do the same thing in the privacy of their home. After asking for and accepting forgiveness, you may want to throw away or burn your list. This symbolic act can reinforce your resolve to be a new person. Of course you may also use your list as you seek forgiveness in the presence of a priest, minister, or friend who understands your need to verbalize your confession.

Whatever you choose to do at this stage, remember that forgiveness is a healing process and that you are called to a new place. In a journal entry, Janet expressed how she felt about this:

> *I have irrevocably turned from my past world view and, as I have turned, I don't know where I am. I leave behind the old world of certainties, and turn to the world of uncertainties.*
>
> *I feel myself creating each new moment and each situation. I do not know where I am. I am happy, but I don't know where to turn. I am between two worlds.*

Feeling that we are standing between two worlds can be painful. Although we are relieved at having confessed, we experience both great uncertainty and great expectancy. Like Janet, we may feel that something worth waiting for is going to happen, but we have no idea what it is.

For many pilgrims, this stage is one of great loneliness. In their writings, they liken it to a tortuous desert where they see only sand and more sand and have no sense of direction. This leads to painful uncertainty, especially for those who have a need to feel in control of their lives. The stage is temporarily a sand trap, a place they want desperately to escape.

Carol felt the pain of the confession stage so intensely that she called me long distance. "I *know* there's something around the corner," she said, "and I'm moving toward it, but I can't see it! I just feel alone!" She cried briefly and then composed herself enough to ask, "Why is it always so painful to move into a new place?"

Although I wasn't able to explain it as well as I wanted on the phone, Carol understood that she would not be stalled at this difficult place forever. She accepted that her confusion and uncertainty were temporary and that one day she would know that this process was part of her journey. A follow-up conversation revealed that soon after talking to me she had, indeed, moved through the pain and on to another stage.

Identifying and verbalizing our sin may bring about a shift of consciousness, which in turn results in a shift of focus. That is, we move from *focusing on the pain that growth involves to focusing on the growth that results from moving through the pain.* This point is subtle but important. Along the pilgrim's way, we all experience "desert times." Some of these times include loneliness or pain or both. At the time, these experiences may seem senseless, but insight will come later. By confessing our sins, we outwardly express a part of ourselves that is transformed by God's power and love.

REFLECTING AND RESPONDING

Do something with your list from yesterday's exercise to symbolize that you have broken with the past and have made a new beginning. In addition to the ways already mentioned, you might plant a flower, shrub, or tree and bury the list in the soil beneath it. Out of wrongs that have been acknowledged and forgiven comes new growth and beauty.

Another ritualizing action is to rip your list into tiny pieces while reflecting on how sin makes us feel pulled apart and scattered. Dispose of the paper and celebrate your new sense of wholeness: take a walk, call a friend, say a prayer of gratitude to a forgiving God.

Think of a way to deal with your list that suits you. In the space provided, write what you plan to do.

Take this action now or sometime before you begin the exercise for Week Four Day Four.

Lay aside the works of darkness
and put on the armor of light.
Romans 13:12

WEEK FOUR, DAY FOUR

PRAYER FOR MY COMPANION ON THE WAY:

I give thanks to you, my God, that I do not travel alone on the journey into a deeper awareness of your love. This week I especially remember _____, who is a pilgrim with me. Amen.

CENTER YOURSELF WITH THIS SCRIPTURE:

Lead me in your truth and teach me,
for you are the God of my salvation;
for you I wait all the day long.
Be mindful of your mercy, Yahweh,
and of your steadfast love,
for they have been from of old.
Remember not the sins of my youth,
or my transgressions;
according to your steadfast love remember me,
because of your goodness, Yahweh!
Psalm 25:5-7, PA

Reading for today:

The Insight Stage

"Oh, now I see...."

At some brief point in our journey an insight leads us to say "That's it!" or "Aha!" or "Oh, now I see." Often it occurs so suddenly that we are at a loss to talk about it or will do so only after a bit of reflection. The insight serves as a reminder that God can always surprise us.

To the person experiencing the insight stage, the revelation has a deep, personal meaning. However, the insight may not seem important to others, and the called-for change might be considered insignificant. But when the insight is our own, the experience is crucial. We know that radical change has to take place before we can proceed on the journey of spiritual growth.

For Jason, a brash, self-centered young man, this stage led him into a time of reflection about who he really was. This excerpt from his journal explains what happened:

> *I began to see clearly that it was not that I wasn't loving and attentive to people, but that I wasn't always aware of them. I guess because of my natural ability to be friendly, people didn't notice that I wasn't always "present" to them. Now I'm more attentive, and that's a radical change for me. I don't know what I expected at this stage, but what I got surely is the answer for me.*

Jason realized what the apostle Paul meant by being transformed by the renewing of our minds (Romans 12:2). At the insight stage, we discover a new person emerging. We are often surprised to look in the mirror and see the same face and same body, because we *know* the interior has been radically changed. Interestingly, the change usually is not at all what we expected.

People who have been at the previous stage (confession) for some time may have built up unrealistic expectations for what is to come. They anticipate a kind of flashy Hollywood production full of special effects. Imaginary scenarios are created around such questions as

- What should I be doing?

- What should God be doing for me?

- Who should be leading me?

The ego builds improbable images of what we think we *should* experience. But instead of a starring role in a major production, we will more likely discover that what God has in mind is more akin to being in a home video! Although this can be disappointing, I seldom find that to be the case. Rather, the insight stage is a humbling experience wherein we realize that most people don't seek first the kingdom of God; they seek first *their place* in the kingdom. The "aha!" comes about when we truly accept that God's kingdom is given to us and that we have no need to worry about our place in it.

The "aha!" came to Donna after she had spent many years working in church and social ministries. Although her work was appreciated, she was active in so many areas that no one recognized her as an expert or specialist in any one thing. When Donna reached her forties, she felt a restlessness that she interpreted as a call to focus her work in a particular area. Here she describes what happened to her at the insight stage:

> *I suddenly saw all my life as ministry, and it had nothing really to do with church or social issues or other people. Instead I saw my ministry as a well of living water within me just bubbling and overflowing.*
>
> *It was no longer a question of "What ministry?" It became a realization that "my life is ministry!" Oh, how dumb I am! Why didn't I see that this was the answer all along?*

Insights often leave us feeling dumb, foolish, or embarrassed, because we believe we "should have known that" at our age or with our experience. Perhaps we did know it, but for some reason we ignored the obvious. Finally God makes it clear. In Donna's case, she came to realize that ministry is not only something you do, it is something you are. Jesus himself *was* ministry. Jesus' whole mission is to make God known and to transfer God's life to us (John 17:1-4).

(The Insight Stage continues on Day 5.)

REFLECTING AND RESPONDING

Again, imagine that the path below is your life. Note the "aha!" experiences you have had. Remember that at the time such experiences occur, we don't always sense God's involvement. But as we develop a deeper awareness of God's presence in our lives, we come to see that God is involved in all our new beginnings and that all new creation is from God.

My Birth

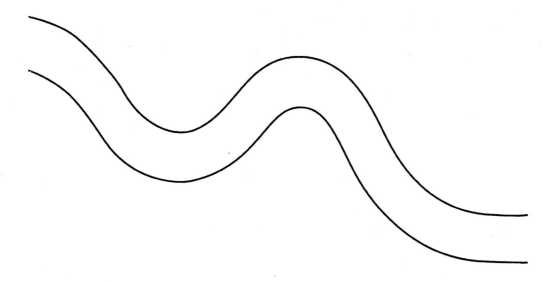

Live, and walk in the way of insight.
Proverbs 9:6

Week Four, Day Five

PRAYER FOR MY COMPANION ON THE WAY:

I give thanks to you, my God, that I do not travel alone on the journey into a deeper awareness of your love. This week I especially remember _____, who is a pilgrim with me. Amen.

CENTER YOURSELF WITH THIS SCRIPTURE:

Lead me in your truth and teach me,
for you are the God of my salvation;
for you I wait all the day long.
Be mindful of your mercy, Yahweh,
and of your steadfast love,
for they have been from of old.
Remember not the sins of my youth,
or my transgressions;
according to your steadfast love remember me,
because of your goodness, Yahweh!
Psalm 25:5-7, PA

READING FOR TODAY:

THE INSIGHT STAGE
(CONTINUED)

Although we pass through each of the stages many times, the insight stage always stands out. Perhaps you have heard it described as a "peak" or "mountaintop" experience. The Bible records many such experiences. I do not think our experiences are so different from Peter's mountaintop experience at the transfiguration. Matthew's account shows Peter's wanting to preserve what happened. However, while Peter is still talking, he is interrupted by God in the bright cloud that envelops them (Matthew 17:1-8).

How often we are like that! We get so busy trying to package and preserve our religious past that God has to interrupt us and make things cloudy. Only upon reflection can we see the brightness of the insight and what God has revealed to us.

So far we have seen how the stages not only lead one into the other but also provide the opportunity to stay where we are, or even move back to where we believe we will be more secure. It is tempting to think of the insight stage as a satisfactory end point when, in fact, the growth we can experience in our relationship with God is endless. Certainly the insight is to be enjoyed, and we don't always have to be "getting somewhere else." But where we are is not where we will always be. More surprises await us.

The insight stage is a good time to look anew at what we expect from our prayers. Many people come to prayer hoping to repeat an experience. I suggest coming to prayer with the attitude that your experience will be entirely new. Let it be a time of thankfulness for what has happened and a time to open yourself to being stretched beyond where you are.

As you look back on your spiritual life, you will recall moments when you experienced a revelation that made you smile and say, "Oh, now I see." That was an awareness of God's time and your time intersecting in a joyful and humbling moment. Celebrate those moments and be assured they will occur again.

REFLECTING AND RESPONDING

Celebrate the "aha!" experiences you identified yesterday on your path of life (see p. 107). Starting with the earliest "aha!" experience you identified, say, "I give thanks for
_____."

Now let the event move into your memory. Put yourself in that time and place: see it, feel it, think about it. When you are ready to move on to the next experience, say, "Thanks be to God."
Do this for as many of the experiences as your time allows.

Let the peace of Christ rule in your hearts. . . .
And be thankful.
Colossians 3:15

Week Four, Day Six

Prayer for my companion on the way:

I give thanks to you, my God, that I do not travel alone on the journey into a deeper awareness of your love. This week I especially remember _____, who is a pilgrim with me. Amen.

Center yourself with this scripture:

Lead me in your truth and teach me,
for you are the God of my salvation;
for you I wait all the day long.
Be mindful of your mercy, Yahweh,
and of your steadfast love,
for they have been from of old.
Remember not the sins of my youth,
or my transgressions;
according to your steadfast love remember me,
because of your goodness, Yahweh!
Psalm 25:5-7, PA

READING FOR TODAY:

THE RELEASE STAGE

"I am giving my power over to God in everyday practical things. . . ."

Frank was a private person who always reminded me of the lone, independent cowboy, determined to be in charge of his own destiny. Although he was a fighter, Frank was slowly losing his life, and there was nothing he could do about it. For one of the first times, he was not in charge.

Soon Frank would be passing over to the risen life. Despite his faith in God, I knew that these final moments were extremely difficult for him. He was not accustomed to giving his power over to anyone, and his struggle was evident to those of us who visited him in the hospital. Finally the time seemed right, and I asked Frank's family if I could be alone with him. They agreed.

With just the two of us in the room, I bent close to Frank and asked if he could hear me. He nodded but did not open his eyes. "Frank," I said very gently, "one of these times will be our last to talk together. I want you to know how much it has meant to me to know you." Frank opened his eyes and looked directly at me. Previously we had talked a lot about his illness. Many times he had told me how tired he was of the pain and of being sick. Now he didn't say a word.

"You've always been a fighter," I said, "but there may come a time soon when you just don't think you can fight any longer. You need to know it's okay to release your power to God and go with Jesus. Jesus will come to you as he has in your dreams. When he does, take his hand and enter into the peace of his loving."

Frank nodded and closed his eyes. "Thanks," he murmured. "Peace. . . ." Then he smiled faintly and I left his room.

To the very end, Frank was stubborn about releasing his grip on power. This is not surprising considering that as Americans we pride ourselves on a history of rugged individualism. The very idea of opening ourselves to another's loving power suggests weakness and inability. This attitude is unfortunate because the release-of-power stage of our spiritual journey represents something quite different. Rather than revealing weakness and inability, the release stage demonstrates strength and ability.

Releasing our grip on power and experiencing God's creative power inspires a feeling of awe. In that regard, this release is similar to the confession stage in which we are aware of how wondrous God is and how sinful we have been. Overwhelmed by

God's love for us, and the fact that we have done nothing to earn that love, we focus on confession. In the release stage we focus on awe. Awe comes from understanding that although we appear insignificant, God is most gracious to us.

Ellen was a young teacher dealing with issues of control. Still at that point in her career where she felt threatened by the children's potential to disrupt her classroom, she feared turning too much control over to them. Some of this same concern about control spilled over into her spiritual life. This is what Ellen wrote in her journal:

> *This whole area of giving my power over was a confusing one to me. But last week I had that tremendous awareness of the "Aha!" in my life. It was as if I was plunged into a pool that was clear and reflecting, the kind in which you can see the whole of the trees on the shore and the sky and sun reflected. Well, I was the pool and I saw the reflection of God in me. . . . It's a strange feeling, because if God were not there I would have nothing to reflect. But also, if I were not here and open to be aware of it, there would be no reflection of God in this place. Maybe that's what the psalms mean by the "fear of the Lord."*

At some point in our lives, most of us probably think of the fear of the Lord as "dread" or "terror." As we mature spiritually, we are better able to see this fear as Ellen saw it—an awesomeness that God intends us to reflect!

I once spent over six months at the release stage and moved on only after an experience that left me awed by the love that is God. I had flown to Denver, Colorado, to see a friend who lived in the mountains outside the city. When we arrived at his home around midnight, there wasn't much to see. The following morning I got up early to pray and slipped quietly downstairs to the living room. When I reached the bottom of the stairs, I felt as if I were still on a plane. Directly ahead of me, outside the glass wall, was a huge mountain. Sunlight made it look like a crystal rainbow. It was one of those larger-than-life experiences that takes your breath away.

In that instant, I had a sense of what it is to be in fear of the Lord, to be in awe of the love that is God. And I asked myself, *Who am I? What significance do I have? What right do I have to exist in the presence of such majesty?* Yet I knew that I was special, as is every person God ever created. If we call to mind that without grains of sand there would be no beach, we realize that our seeming insignificance makes us significant.

Standing there watching the early morning light bathe the mountain landscape, I released my compulsive need for control to God. As I did so, this scripture rang in my ears: "Those who trust in the Lord are like Mount Zion, which cannot be shaken but stands fast for ever. As the hills enfold Jerusalem, so the Lord enfolds his people, now and evermore" (Psalm 125, NEB).

Each time we pass through the release stage, we die to some part of ourselves that stubbornly wants to be in control and prevents us from understanding our true relationship to God. In these times of resistance, it helps to remember that even Jesus released his need to control into God's loving power.

A highly successful young lawyer I know understands both how important and how necessary it is to release the need for power. Professionally he enjoys considerable power and finds it important to take time to keep his life in perspective. After reviewing his experiences in the release stage, he made this entry in his journal:

> *The implications of giving my power over are daily, I have discovered. It seems that I have become aware, time and time again, that I can give up some of my need to control. And I discover that this places me in a position of waiting again. I know that something is going to happen. I just don't know when.*
>
> *So I went to the woods today and again was aware of how awesome my God is. This is really a stage of growth that I can reflect upon and see that, in fact, I am giving my power over to God in everyday practical things.*

What about you? Do you find yourself trying to go it alone and be in charge? Or are your senses open to hear the call to release your need for ultimate control so that God might more readily be reflected in what you say and do?

REFLECTING AND RESPONDING

What has been your understanding of the "fear of the Lord"?

_____

_____

_____

_____

When have you experienced the fear of the Lord?

_____

_____

_____

_____

What is your experience of awe before God?

_____

_____

_____

_____

What difference do you see between awe and fear?

_____

_____

_____

_____

Your steadfast love is higher than the heavens,
and your faithfulness reaches to the clouds.
Be exalted, O God, above the heavens,
and let your glory be over the earth.
Psalm 108:4-5

Preparation for the Group Meeting

This week's group meeting will include a celebration service to remember the "ahas!" of life.

- Reflect on your "ahas!" and pick one that you would like to share with the group. (You will be doing as a group what you did alone in "Reflecting and Responding" on Day 5.) In turn each person will say, "I give thanks for _____" (naming a particular "aha!"). The group will respond, "Thanks be to God!"

- Remember to bring this book to the group meeting. You may want to refer to something you read or wrote during the week.

Some people find it helpful and more comfortable when sharing with a group to read something they have written prior to the meeting. If this is true for you, use this page or a separate piece of paper and write out what you want to share at the weekly meeting.

_____

_____

_____

_____

_____

Fifth Group Meeting

PURPOSE:

To share experiences of the past week and celebrate "aha!" experiences.

MATERIALS NEEDED:

- Name tags if they seem necessary

- Bible, candle with a sturdy base, plant or fresh flowers

- Watch or timer

- 3 x 5 index card for each member of the group with his or her name on it (Make new cards if they were not saved from the previous week's meeting.)

PREPARATIONS:

- Arrange the seating so people can see one another easily.

- Create a focus table with the Bible, candle, and plant or flowers. Have the Bible open and the candle lit as people arrive.

PROCEDURE:

If anybody brought something that symbolizes their journey of the spirit, they may place it on the focus table. (Those who brought symbols will have an opportunity to tell the group about them during the discussion time. Others may wish to describe something that is a symbol for them.)

➤ 1. Begin by praying together the following scripture that all have prayed throughout the week:

Lead me in your truth and teach me,
for you are the God of my salvation;
for you I wait all the day long.
Be mindful of your mercy, Yahweh,
and of your steadfast love,
for they have been from of old.
Remember not the sins of my youth,
or my transgressions;
according to your steadfast love remember me,
because of your goodness, Yahweh!
Psalm 25:5-7, PA

➤ 2. Follow with three minutes of silence. (Use a watch or timer.) Ask that the members of the group reflect on their experiences during the week:

- a particular learning, insight, or discovery;

- a story from the text with which they especially identified;

- God's presence in their lives this week.

➤ 3. Initiate group sharing. Invite anyone who has something to share to do so. If no one responds, use these questions to stimulate discussion. It's not necessary to cover all the questions. Because different people relate to different questions, it's helpful to read them all and then wait for someone to begin. At some meetings the entire time for discussion may be spent on just one question.

- How have you experienced God's presence this week?

- What particular learning or insight did you gain?

- What do you do when you find yourself wanting to be "in charge"?

- Did most of your "ahas!" take place when you were alone or in the company of others?

End the discussion ten minutes before the close of your meeting. This allows time for picking new prayer companions and the closing ritual. So as not to end the discussion abruptly, give a five-minute warning by saying, "We have five minutes of discussion time left."

➤ 4. Pick new names for prayer companions. Place the 3 x 5 cards face down and mix them up. Each person draws a name; those who get their own draw again. Ask group members to write their new prayer companion's name in their workbooks.

➤ 5. Suggest that the group members take one minute in silence to think about the "aha!" experience they want to share. (Use a watch or timer.) Begin the sharing by saying, "I give thanks for_____" and mention your own "aha!" After each individual's sharing, the group responds, "Thanks be to God."

➤ 6. End by praying the regular closing prayer together:

Thank you, God, for bringing us together
on this spiritual journey.
Light our way as we travel the road
that brings us closer to you.
Be with us to celebrate our triumphs
and encourage us when we grow weary.
Wherever we are on the pilgrim's way,
grant us the grace to feel your presence
and to know that your love is always with us.
Amen.

WEEK FIVE, DAY ONE

PRAYER FOR MY COMPANION ON THE WAY:

I give thanks to you, my God, that I do not travel alone on the journey into a deeper awareness of your love. This week I especially remember _____, who is a pilgrim with me. Amen.

CENTER YOURSELF WITH THIS SCRIPTURE:

> I will give thanks to the Lord
> with my whole heart;
> I will tell of all your wonderful deeds.
> I will be glad and exult in you;
> I will sing praise to your
> name, O Most High.
> Psalm 9:1-2

Reading for today:

The Expectation Stage

"I know that it will happen, but I really don't know when. . . ."

The temperature was in the high eighties, and the humidity seemed even higher as a group of friends and I stood outside the church talking. When Paul, a fellow parishioner, pulled his car up close to the sidewalk, we all turned to watch. His wife Pam was already a week overdue with their first child, and as she struggled to get out of the car, her discomfort was obvious. But with a smile on her face, she turned to us and quipped, "Please pray for deliverance for me!"

Pam was at the "but when?" stage of her pregnancy, certain her child would be born soon but not knowing exactly when. A comparison can be made between Pam's experience with pregnancy and the expectation stage of our spiritual journey. This stage is also a period of waiting during which we experience discomfort. Mostly, though, it is a period of hope because we know for certain that something new is coming into our life.

Each time I am at this stage and glance in a mirror, I see something different about myself. Perhaps no one else sees it, but I am reminded of that old saying, "You look like the cat that just swallowed the canary!" *Pleased. Satisfied. Full.* The words help explain my experience but do not adequately express my feelings. Perhaps this line from the psalms most adequately reflects what it is like to be in the expectation stage: "Truly my heart waits silently for God" (Psalm 62:5, NEB).

Jim was married, happy with his life, and passing from one stage to another with a rapidity I don't often see. In his journal he expressed the expectation stage with clarity:

> Now I guess the question is, "But when will this happen?" I see that I have moved along a particular path, and I find myself out of control. It's as if I have to sit and wait until it happens. I feel what it must be like being pregnant and knowing that the time is near but not really knowing when. You keep looking for the signs, and even make them up and make them into more than they are. Is this the way it is supposed to be? Is this what Peter was experiencing when he always seemed to be a jump ahead of Jesus in what was supposed to happen? I guess I really can enjoy this time of waiting before God.

Although Jim passed quickly through many of the stages, other pilgrims find their journey quite different. At forty-three, Janet was a successful therapist who felt herself moving slowly but definitely moving. Though she was extremely busy in her practice, she took time to journal, and over a period of three years she shared her journal with me. This entry reflects the cycling and recycling of the stages from the point of view of someone at the expectation stage:

> *Is it forever that I have been waiting for all of this to come together? Each time I pray, I remind myself that I pray not to achieve anything but to be faithful in responding to God. . . . I see that it doesn't matter if I want to pray or not—any more than it matters if I want to breathe. I will because I have chosen to respond to God's call for me. . . . Even though I have recalled times in the past when I have thought,* This time too shall pass and I will move into getting it all together, *still it is waiting and asking,* "But when, O Lord, but when?"

At this point in our journey, we have a tremendous urge to control time: How we would like to rush it along. How we would like to have more of it. How we misuse the time we already have. But the only way we can control time is to make the best possible use of the time we already have.

(The expectation stage continues on Day 2.)

REFLECTING AND RESPONDING

We all have expectations—expectations of ourselves, of others, and of God. If we begin with negative expectations, negative outcomes tend to follow. On the contrary, if our expectations are positive, we are more likely to have positive outcomes. Writing affirming statements helps us think well of ourselves and anticipate that good things will happen in our lives. Add other affirming statements to these:

I am a child of God.
There is a divine plan of goodness for me.
As I seek guidance from God, I am led.

_____

_____

_____

_____

_____

_____

_____

_____

I can do all things through him who strengthens me.
Philippians 4:13

Week Five, Day Two

Prayer for my companion on the way:

I give thanks to you, my God, that I do not travel alone on the journey into a deeper awareness of your love. This week I especially remember _____, who is a pilgrim with me. Amen.

Center yourself with this scripture:

I will give thanks to the Lord
with my whole heart;
I will tell of all your wonderful deeds.
I will be glad and exult in you;
I will sing praise to your
name, O Most High.
Psalm 9:1-2

READING FOR TODAY:

THE EXPECTATION STAGE
(CONTINUED)

I can recall the exact moment I decided it was not worth living my life on a tight schedule. Years ago, I had a job that involved traveling by air about sixty percent of the time. I would land in a city and within an hour have rented a car and driven downtown for a meeting. I was not alone in this experience. In the business world, thousands of people travel this way each day, often making two or more cities in a twenty-four hour period.

One day as I was sitting in O'Hare airport in Chicago, I heard racing footsteps. I looked up and saw a man who was running hard, obviously trying to make his flight. He had an attache case in his hand and a garment bag flung over his shoulder. Because of the many times I too had raced to catch a plane, I identified with this man. Those times when I didn't make my connection, I would often lose whole days that somehow had to be made up.

As the man got to the ticket counter near me, he gasped for breath and asked, "Did the plane for L.A. leave yet?"

"No," the agent said, "you still have time."

The man sighed and slapped his side. "Great! I made it!" Then he grabbed at his chest and slumped to the floor. He was dead.

That day I decided that living on such a tight schedule was not worth it. From then on, my concept of time changed. I began to see that all time is sacred, not just those moments that fit our schedules. Since then I have learned to move more gently with time. Now I work with it instead of *against* it, and I enjoy the moments I used to waste.

In so many areas of our lives, we try to hurry up time and get on with the action. One of the important things we learn during the expectation stage is to appreciate the moments of waiting. In his journal, a young runner named Edward brings the various sensations of this stage into focus:

> *It's like running in a race for me. This stage of asking "but when?" is like a certain point in a race. I begin to sense that it's all going to come out well. I feel scattered and anxious; I know that it will happen, but I really don't know when.*

The hope of this stage is certain to be fulfilled, because after spiritual labor, as in pregnancy, something new enters our life. This does not happen according to our schedule, but comes about in due time.

Reflecting and Responding

"What's new?" is a familiar expression. What newness do you want to enter your life: New attitude? New beginning? New awareness? New discipline? New insight? Finish this prayer, stating the newness you want for yourself.

With God I can create new . . .

_____

_____

_____

_____

_____

_____

_____

Whatever you ask for in prayer with faith,
you will receive.
Matthew 21:22

Week Five, Day Three

PRAYER FOR MY COMPANION ON THE WAY:

I give thanks to you, my God, that I do not travel alone on the journey into a deeper awareness of your love. This week I especially remember _____, who is a pilgrim with me. Amen.

CENTER YOURSELF WITH THIS SCRIPTURE:

I will give thanks to the Lord
with my whole heart;
I will tell of all your wonderful deeds.
I will be glad and exult in you;
I will sing praise to your
name, O Most High.
Psalm 9:1-2

READING FOR TODAY:

The Integration Stage

"I have come to be comfortable with myself. . . ."

What happens when we suddenly recognize that life is coming together for us? Over time we have gone through the stages and laid the groundwork. Then comes that moment when all the telltale signs of the birthing have taken place and we look at what has happened within us. What we see is a new creation. Hard as it is to believe, this potential was within us all along, being nurtured and growing. Now it has become real and tangible outside ourselves.

For me, awareness of this integration occurs in the latter part of the expectation stage. Again and again, I get hints that the time is near. These hints are like mild labor pains at first, followed by hard contractions. Usually confirmation that this is indeed the awaited moment comes from someone else. But for my wife, Eleanor, the confirmation seems to come from within. Frequently, she experiences these times while out running and returns to the house wearing a knowing smile. Then she goes directly to her journal, and I know that I must wait until that entry is made before I hear her tale of discovery. Often I feel I have to work hard to get my answers, while all she has to do is go out and run! Although I tell others that everyone receives insights in different ways, it took me a long time to accept the truth of this in my own life.

Many people expect this stage of the journey to be dramatic—maybe something comparable to a burst of fireworks in a night sky or the intensity of a full orchestra. Sometimes it is like that. But more likely it will be a quiet realization such as the one Susan, a young actress and director, expressed in her journal:

> *Having everything come together like this while I have someone with whom to talk is great. I suspect that I wouldn't really reflect on these things if I were alone. I expected some great Broadway production finale when actually it happened rather quietly and deeply within. Beautiful.*

For Susan, and for many others, the integration happens as if hands were laid upon their eyes. The scales fall away, letting them see anew. This is the type of experience we celebrate when we sing, "I once was lost and now I'm found, was blind, but now I see."

Because integrating experiences are usually preceded by times of waiting and quiet, people have difficulty pinpointing them. Also, we become impatient with waiting and instead of persevering the full time, we return to a previous stage. Then we find ourselves saying, "You know, it seems as if I've been at this point many times before." Well, of course we have! Each time that our impatience hinders the integration, we move into a stage where we have already been.

Think about your own journey and look carefully at those times when you wanted to give up and say, "It's not worth it" or "It will never happen to me." Now you see how important it was to have patience and wait out the discouragement with prayer and a calm spirit.

Scripture tells us we are to be perfect as God is perfect. As we discussed earlier, the word *perfect* as it is used in this context means together or integrated or whole. This puts perfection within reach; it is possible to be whole and at peace. Marian, a forty-two-year-old woman, tells how this stage of her journey involved developing a sense of self-worth. In her journal she wrote:

> *How can I describe "knowing" that I am loved and having my life come together like this? Everything from the past week has pointed to this, yet I didn't see it all fall into place until this morning. The dreams that I have been having, the insights, were part of this great "getting it together."*
>
> *I have come to be comfortable with myself for the first time I can ever remember. I guess the secret is that I love me and it doesn't really matter who else does.*

(The integration stage continues on Day 4.)

REFLECTING AND RESPONDING

Jesus instructed that we love our neighbor as we love ourselves. The key here is "as we love ourselves." Before we can like and accept others, we need to like and accept who we are. Most of us, however, are quicker to focus on our weaknesses and perceived limitations than on our strengths and possibilities. But if we are to live to the fullness of our potential, we need to emphasize our strengths and use them constructively. Perhaps then—like Marian in the reading for today—we will be comfortable with ourselves, knowing that in both our strength and in our weakness, we have God's unconditional love.

These are my strengths: (Circle those that apply to you. Add others not included here.)

Faith	Perseverance	Patience
Ambition	Honesty	Cheerfulness
Listening	Optimism	Helpfulness
Generosity	Leadership	

Others:

_____

_____

_____

_____

These are strengths I admire in others and would like to develop in myself:

_____

_____

_____

_____

There are varieties of gifts, but the same Spirit;
and there are varieties of services,
but the same Lord.
1 Corinthians 12:4-5

Week Five, Day Four

Prayer for my companion on the way:

I give thanks to you, my God, that I do not travel alone on the journey into a deeper awareness of your love. This week I especially remember _____, who is a pilgrim with me. Amen.

Center yourself with this scripture:

I will give thanks to the Lord
with my whole heart;
I will tell of all your wonderful deeds.
I will be glad and exult in you;
I will sing praise to your
name, O Most High.
Psalm 9:1-2

Reading for today:

The Integration Stage
(continued)

The integration stage is like putting the last piece of a jigsaw puzzle in place. When we see the entire picture of our journey, we have a sense of accomplishment and feel complete. We then understand that all our preparation for wholeness occurred along the way.

Naturally, we want this unifying experience to last forever. We want to always feel integrated and whole, but this stage is not eternal in the sense that we do not arrive and stay there a lifetime. We will have integrating experiences throughout our life, and each time it will be as if another plant has bloomed in our garden or another room has been added to our house.

Often roadblocks to feeling whole have roots in childhood. This was true for Don, who had been involved in many high-powered renewal movements. He recorded this insight in his journal:

> After thirty-three years, I see clearly that the emotions which resulted
> from my previous encounters with God were so strong because I always
> wanted to be touched by my father as an act of acknowledgment and
> love. Then the thought came to me that perhaps Jesus was telling me
> I would feel his presence if I would first feel my own true presence.

Seeing a connection with childhood, as Don did—or identifying another experience from our past—can open us to a peace never felt before. We can also open up to this peace by identifying some persistent or recurring need or truth about ourselves. Yet often we are reluctant to face those things that strike at the heart of us. The story of the woman at the well is an effective illustration. When the Samaritan woman came to draw water, Jesus engaged her in conversation (John 4:5-30). Each time he revealed more to her about her life, or answered a deep yet unfulfilled need, she experienced a greater understanding of herself and continued to open like a bud come to bloom. How like her we are!

In helping people with their spiritual direction, I am amazed—and often in grace-filled awe—to see how God's revealing power brings light and truth out of the dark places of their lives. I might ask, "Can you remember another time when you felt like this?"

There is usually a long, thoughtful pause before the person says, "Yes, I remember feeling like this not only one time but many times. Maybe there's a key to understanding this after all!"

At other times questions are met with great hesitation, even avoidance. For whatever reason—often because it is not yet time—we detour around learning the truth about our own lives. But when we seek in honesty (perhaps with the help of a spiritual adviser) the truth emerges for us. The discovery may amaze us and like the Samaritan woman, we rush about saying, "Wait until I tell you what I discovered about myself!"

The surprising response we often get is, "I'm glad you finally saw that!"

(The integration stage continues on Day 5.)

REFLECTING AND RESPONDING

All along the path of your journey in *The Hunger of the Heart* program, you have been making discoveries about yourself. Summarize at least one of those discoveries.

_____

_____

_____

How are you integrating this discovery into your life?

_____

_____

_____

How is it contributing to your feeling of wholeness?

_____

_____

_____

What impact will it have on your family? friends?

_____

_____

_____

_____

Live as children of light—for the fruit of the light
is found in all that is good and right and true.
Ephesians 5:8-9

Week Five, Day Five

PRAYER FOR MY COMPANION ON THE WAY:

I give thanks to you, my God, that I do not travel alone on the journey into a deeper awareness of your love. This week I especially remember _____, who is a pilgrim with me. Amen.

CENTER YOURSELF WITH THIS SCRIPTURE:

I will give thanks to the Lord
with my whole heart;
I will tell of all your wonderful deeds.
I will be glad and exult in you;
I will sing praise to your
name, O Most High.
Psalm 9:1-2

The Integration Stage
(continued)

At one point in my life I was eagerly awaiting an integrating moment of insight and peace. I was a young man anxious to find answers when I heard that Father P., a professor from India, was a wise spiritual adviser. At the time he lived in California, and I was living in Florida. When a business trip took me to California, I decided to stay an extra day and rent a car to go see him. I wrote for an appointment, and his secretary responded, saying he could meet with me at four on the day I suggested, and that I was invited to stay for dinner. Needless to say, I was overjoyed.

After driving for two hours, I arrived at the scheduled time only to find that Father P. was not home. A guest at the house who spoke virtually no English (and I knew nothing of his east Indian dialect) greeted me at the door and invited me in.

The houseguest and I sat in semisilence for more than an hour. During this time I became restless, then annoyed. *Who did Father P. think he was to keep me waiting like this? After I had made such an effort to be here, he should be able to keep his appointment.*

An hour and a half after I arrived, Father P. whisked into the room. With a few brief words of apology, he ushered me into his library and seated himself behind a large desk. He invited me to take a chair in front of the desk. Then he said, "Begin."

Begin I did. For two hours I emptied myself to this man, telling him everything I felt he needed to know in order to give me the ultimate answer. When I finished, he got up and came from behind the desk. Taking a chair, he put it in front of me and sat so close that our knees were touching. "Now," he directed, "pay attention."

My heart drummed and my mouth went dry. I was certain he was going to touch my forehead or my heart. Then instant sanctity, or at least enlightenment, would be mine. He leaned forward as if to touch me, and I held my breath. This was it! Like a gentle, loving grandfather, he pointed his right index finger at me and said, "Pray unceasingly, go home, love your wife and children, and do what needs to be done. Now let's go eat!" Rising abruptly, he led me to the dining room.

Stunned, I followed along. *For this advice—this enlightenment—I had gone to so much trouble?* I sat at the table feeling angry, tired, annoyed, confused. Throughout the meal Father P. conversed sporadically with his houseguest in a language foreign to me. After taking my leave and making the two-hour drive to my hotel, I wanted to write what I was feeling and thinking but was unable to do so.

Back home the next day, I told Eleanor every detail of the story. When I finished, her gaze held fast to mine as she said, "Thank God someone finally told you that!"

Sometimes we are the last ones to know the truth about ourselves. I see now that this wise man's advice was one of the great coming-together moments of my life. His words were right for me, and I find that with a bit of adaptation they can be applied to anyone's life. Whatever our age or circumstance, we can pray and we can love. And when we do that, we will grow spiritually and get on with what needs to be done.

REFLECTING AND RESPONDING

"Bloom where you're planted" is an expression familiar to many of us. What can you do right where you are to let the love of God shine through you and into the lives of others? Be specific.

Family member(s):

_____

_____

_____

_____

Friend(s):

_____

_____

_____

_____

Coworker(s):

_____

_____

_____

_____

Neighbor(s):

_____

_____

_____

_____

Other(s):

_____

_____

_____

For in fact, the kingdom of God is among us.
Luke 17:21

WEEK FIVE, DAY SIX

PRAYER FOR MY COMPANION ON THE WAY:

I give thanks to you, my God, that I do not travel alone on the journey into a deeper awareness of your love. This week I especially remember _____, who is a pilgrim with me. Amen.

CENTER YOURSELF WITH THIS SCRIPTURE:

I will give thanks to the Lord
with my whole heart;
I will tell of all your wonderful deeds.
I will be glad and exult in you;
I will sing praise to your
name, O Most High.
Psalm 9:1-2

READING FOR TODAY:

GOING ON

"Each journey is both the same and different. . . ."

And so, we come to the end. The end, however, is not the end, because after experiencing a time of wholeness we find ourselves moving once more through the awakening and seeking stages of the spiritual journey. Each journey is both the same and different: the same because we will once again cover familiar ground while seeking or experiencing doubts or wondering what lies ahead; different because we now have a history against which to compare and contrast what happens to us.

The original awakening that leads to a greater concern about spiritual growth is like a stone dropped into the water of our life. The first few ripples are distinct, but as they move farther and farther out they become less distinguishable. Nevertheless, the ripples are still there. So it is as we pass through the stages time and time again. The earlier passings may dim, but the impressions remain.

Arthur was in his mid thirties and had grown up with the idea that religion should be as steadfast and unyielding as a rock. He liked to think that once you reach a certain stage of spiritual growth you are complete and should be happy just to rest there. However, when he examined his attentiveness to God in more detail, he discovered that spirituality is not static but rather always changing and growing. Arthur reflected on this in his journal:

> It is helpful to understand that I have recycled—passed through the stages again—at least twice and am able to accept that. I have had feelings of guilt and anger for not staying in one place and have felt as if I was backsliding. Now I know it's not backsliding, it's simply integrating experiences at deeper levels and then going on.

Arthur's concern about backsliding is common. In the early months and years of spiritual growth, pilgrims on the way fail to realize that the principle of one-step-forward, two-steps-back idea is false here. Even when we choose to remain where we are, or return to a more secure place, we are still in a movement toward God. Bear in mind that spiritual growth is not like the rungs of a ladder that we climb, but rather like the growth rings of a tree. With us as with trees, growth varies from year to year.

What looks like backsliding often appears in retrospect to have been a necessary preparation for more complete understanding. Remember Peter's denial on the eve of the crucifixion (Luke 22:54-62)? At first glance, it would seem to be a step backward, but within the total picture Peter moved into a deeper commitment when Jesus asked, "Do you love me?" (John 21:15-17). The fact that Jesus asks the question three times undoubtedly heightens Peter's awareness of the times he declared his love for Jesus and then denied him. The depth of Peter's sorrow over the denial was probably surpassed only by the love he felt when Jesus said, "Feed my sheep" (John 21:17).

Likewise, Paul's witnessing the death of Stephen and working to destroy the church seemed to be a step backward on his personal journey (see Acts 8:1). Instead it was another step for Paul along the way to the Damascus road experience (Acts 9:1-6).

All our experiences provide fertile ground for God to plant seeds of faith and bring forth new fruit. Our growth with God, in turn, becomes ministry to others. We see this clearly in the examples of Peter and Paul. From their own failings came insights on the importance and focus of their ministry. We are like them. Our prayer life and our spiritual growth will lead us to a greater understanding of our role in ministering to others whether it be in our family, our neighborhood, our work, or the wider world.

I find that those people who most yearn for God often have the greatest feelings of failure. Many people do not believe that God loves them unconditionally, so in order to be worthy of that love, they set difficult to impossible goals—goals they feel they must attain to be worthy of God's love. When they do not reach the goals, they see only their failure, their backsliding. They do not realize that the strivings themselves make the ground more fertile for the seeds of new life and ministry.

At fifty-eight, Robert was an architect with many clients and a busy life that included a family of grown children. Although he had been attentive to his spiritual life, he had not been able to make sense out of what he saw as a hodgepodge of experiences. Understanding that there were stages that could be passed through over and over gave him a practical way to make sense of his lifepath. In his journal he wrote:

> *In all areas of my life I am at different places in the stages of growth: at home with my family, at the office, in my life plans, in my inner life of prayer. No wonder I'm feeling scattered. I guess the thing to do is . . . place my priorities where I need to in order to get all the areas in the same general place on my journey.*

The stages of spiritual growth serve each of us in a somewhat different way. They are first of all guidelines to help make sense out of the yearnings, the doubts, the anger, and the wonder that enter the life of every Christian. The stages are also a means to see where we are today, where we were yesterday, and where we hope to be tomorrow. Most of all, the stages help us appreciate that there is no particular place we must "get to"; there is only a life to live. God calls us to wholeness, to live as Jesus lived and to love as Jesus loved. As we earnestly strive to do that, we find that the hunger of the heart is satisfied.

REFLECTING AND RESPONDING

During the course of this program, you have done a path of life exercise at three different stages of your journey. On this last day of reflecting and responding, turn back to those exercises (pp. 18, 86, 107). In reviewing your responses to each of them, ask yourself

- What patterns of behavior do I see emerging?

- What does where I've been tell me about where I want to go?

- What connections do I see between other people and the progress of my journey?

In the journey of the spirit, the overriding theme is one of continuing—of "going on." At times we may walk blindly; at other times we stumble. And if we visit a place we've already been, we may even think we are going backward. But in fact, we are not because in revisiting those places we see them in a new light and are better able to respond with creativity and love.

Throughout *The Hunger of the Heart* program you have looked at various aspects of your life. Although at times this may have produced painful emotions, along with them I suspect that joy, peace and humor surfaced as well. My hope is that these weeks in the program have encouraged you on your journey, and that the support you received from other pilgrims on the way has helped satisfy your hunger of the heart.

Be doers of the word, and not merely hearers.

James 1:22

PREPARATION FOR THE GROUP MEETING

This will be your last meeting with the group. As in previous meetings, you will be discussing your experiences and reflections during the past week. Time will also be allowed to discuss the entire program and what it has meant to you. Use these questions to help in your review:

- What story, paragraph, or line in the text did you find especially meaningful? (Mark it so you can find it easily.)

- How have you been aware of God's presence in your life this past week?

  _____

  _____

  _____

  _____

- What has *The Hunger of the Heart* program meant to you?

  _____

  _____

  _____

  _____

- What practical ways can you live into your learnings and discoveries?

  _____

  _____

  _____

  _____

Sixth Group Meeting

Purpose:

To share experiences and celebrate being part of *The Hunger of the Heart* program.

Materials needed:

- Bible, candle with a sturdy base, plant or fresh flowers

- Watch or timer

- Anything that would help celebrate the end of the program

Preparations:

- Arrange the seating so people can see one another easily.

- Create a focus table with the Bible, candle, and plant or flowers. Have the Bible open and the candle lit as people arrive. Include flowers or a plant as a symbol of growth and change.

Procedure:

If anybody brought something that symbolizes their journey of the spirit, they may place it on the focus table. (Those who brought symbols will have an opportunity to tell the group about them during the discussion time. Others may wish to describe something that is a symbol for them.)

➤ 1. Begin by praying together the following scripture that all have prayed throughout the week:

I will give thanks to the Lord
with my whole heart;
I will tell of all your wonderful deeds.
I will be glad and exult in you;
I will sing praise to your
name, O Most High.
Psalm 9:1-2

➤ 2. Follow with three minutes of silence. (Use a watch or timer.) Ask that members of the group reflect on their experiences during the week:

- a particular learning, insight, or discovery;

- a story from the reading with which they especially identified;

- God's presence in their lives this week.

➤ 3. Initiate group sharing. Because this is the last meeting, shorten the usual discussion time by half to allow time to reflect on and celebrate being pilgrims on the way. Ask:

- How have you experienced God's presence this week?

- What particular learning or insight did you gain?

So as not to end the discussion abruptly, give a five-minute warning by saying, "We have five minutes of discussion time left."

➤ 4. Have one minute of silence. (Use a watch or timer.) In that time of silence, ask group members to reflect on

- a particular time of grace, insight, or "aha!",

- how the program contributed to their journey of the spirit,

- practical steps they can take to continue the journey.

After the minute of silence, ask people to share their reflections.

➤ 5. End the meeting by praying the regular closing prayer together:

Thank you, God, for bringing us together
on this spiritual journey.
Light our way as we travel the road
that brings us closer to you.
Be with us to celebrate our triumphs
and encourage us when we grow weary.
Wherever we are on the pilgrim's way,
grant us the grace to feel your presence
and to know that your love is always with us.
Amen.

Appendix

The Breath Prayer

Prayer is the cornerstone of spiritual life. Among the many forms of prayer is one known as the breath prayer. This prayer takes its name from the Hebrew word *ruach* which can be translated as "wind," "breath," or "spirit." The *ruach* of God hovered over the waters of chaos in creation (Genesis 1:2) and God breathed the breath of life into all living beings (Genesis 2:7). Because this way of praying reminds us that we share God's breath, and because it comes as easily and naturally as breathing, it is known as the breath prayer.

This ancient form of prayer is found in writings as early as the second century. Perhaps the best known breath prayer is the one called the Jesus Prayer: "Lord Jesus Christ, Son of God, have mercy on me, a sinner." The Jesus prayer originated in the Christian tradition of the East and can be traced back to the sixth century. At that time, monks and others who were seeking a deeper relationship with God sought a disciplined form of prayer they could pray anywhere and at anytime. This brief prayer encompassed all one needed to believe in order to be saved. Over time the Jesus prayer was abbreviated to "Lord Jesus Christ, have mercy," and even "Jesus, mercy."

The approach to the breath prayer I suggest is like those ancient prayers of praise and petition that have been such an integral part of our Christian tradition. Instead of using other people's words, we each discover our own breath prayer. This prayer arises from our deepest need and gives us a way to follow the apostle Paul's admonishment to "pray without ceasing" (1 Thessalonians 5:17, KJV). Just as breathing supports life and renews our physical body, unceasing prayer keeps us attentive to God's presence and renews our spirit. To discover your breath prayer, follow these simple steps:

STEP 1

Sit comfortably and calm yourself. Close your eyes and be mindful that you are in God's loving presence. Recall a passage from scripture that places you in a peaceful frame of mind. "Be still, and know that I am God" (Psalm 46:10) is a verse that many people find calming.

STEP 2

With your eyes still closed, imagine that God is calling you by name. Hear God's asking, "(Your name), what do you want?"

STEP 3

Answer God directly with whatever comes honestly from your heart. Your answer may be no more than a single word, such as *peace* or *love* or *forgiveness*. Your answer might instead be a phrase or a brief sentence, such as "I want to feel your forgiveness" or "I want to know your love." Whatever your response, it will be at the heart of your prayer. You may "want" many things, but wants can be narrowed to your deepest yearning that is basic to your spiritual well-being. The question to be asked is *What do I want that will make me feel most whole?*

STEP 4

Choose your favorite name or image for God. Choices people commonly make include God, Shepherd, Jesus, Spirit, Living Fire, Creator, Lord, Christ, Eternal Light.

STEP 5

Combine your name for God with your answer to God's question "What do you want?" and you have your prayer. For example:

What I want	Name I call God	Possible Prayer
rest	Shepherd	My Shepherd, let me rest in thee.
to be led	Eternal Light	Lead me on my way, Eternal Light.
love	Jesus	Jesus, let me feel your love.

If several ideas occur, write down the various possibilities and then eliminate and/or combine ideas until you have focused your prayer. Once you get at the heart of your yearning, search for words that give it expression. Then work with these words until you have a prayer of six to eight syllables that flows smoothly when spoken aloud or expressed silently as heart-thoughts. When you achieve a feeling of wholeness, serenity will deepen and flow into all areas of your life.

Some prayers are most rhythmic when God's name is placed at the beginning. Others require it at the end. When your prayer seems right for you, use it again and again throughout the day. In time it will come as easily and naturally as breathing and you will be answering Scripture's call to pray unceasingly.

For a more in-depth look at prayer, and this form of prayer in particular, refer to my book, *The Breath of Life: A Simple Way to Pray,* and the *Breath of Life Workbook* published by Upper Room Books.